VOLLEYBALL

about the authors

Glen H. Egstrom, Ph.D., is a Professor of Kinesiology at the University of California at Los Angeles. During the past twenty-five years, he has taught a variety of courses including exercise physiology, applied anatomy, environmental physiology, aquatic kinesiology, biomechanical analysis and conditioning for optimal performance. He is a fellow in the American College of Sports Medicine and holds memberships in AAHPER, the Undersea Medical Society and the Marine Technology Society. He has authored many articles on human performance research above and below the water. A book on Human Movement has been published and chapters have been contributed to books on underwater medicine and diving safety. He has also given over 400 public lectures on various aspects of human performance research during the past twelve years. Work with students has resulted in the development of training and conditioning programs for the specific requirements of a wide variety of sports interests including volleyball, swimming, scuba diving and other aquatic sports.

Frances Schaafsma is a Professor of Physical Education and Associate Director of Sports, Athletics, and Recreation at California State University, Long Beach. She earned her bachelor's and master's degrees at California State, Long Beach and her Ph.D. at the University of Southern California. Dr. Schaafsma coached varsity volleyball at CSULB from 1962 through 1971 and women's varsity basketball from 1962 through 1979. Dr. Schaafsma has been active in women's sports as a player, official and coach. She has served in numerous elected and appointed positions in women's sports organizations, including the first commissioner for the National Championship of the Commission for Intercollegiate Athletics for Women from 1968 through 1970. She is the immediate past president for the Western Association for Intercollegiate Athletics for Women. She has also conducted coaching clinics in volleyball throughout the United States. Dr. Schaafsma has authored two books published by Wm. C. Brown Company Publishers: *Basketball for Women* and *Volleyball for Coaches and Teachers* as well as co-authoring *Volleyball*.

VOLLEYBALL
Third Edition

Physical Education Activities Series

GLEN H. EGSTROM
University of California, Los Angeles

FRANCES SCHAAFSMA
California State University, Long Beach

Photography by Lynne Farrell and Terri Murphy

wcb

Wm. C. Brown Company Publishers
Dubuque, Iowa

Consulting Editors

Physical Education
Aileene Lockhart
Texas Woman's University

Parks and Recreation
David Gray
California State University, Long Beach

Health
Robert Kaplan
The Ohio State University

**Physical Education Activities
Evaluation Materials Editor**

Jane A. Mott
Texas Woman's University

contents

preface

This text is intended to provide an interested neophyte with the understandings and skill descriptions which will lead to effective, efficient play. We want the reader to be able to enjoy the game to the fullest extent possible while undergoing the transition necessary to become a skilled volleyball player.

To make skill development fun, this text concentrates upon fundamentals and the progression from simple to more complex skill levels. It is a basic text in the sport and is organized to help the student move in logical progressions in both skill and understanding. The third edition also incorporates a significantly improved set of illustrative materials which should enable the reader to gain a clearer insight into the various skills and strategies.

The current rules and philosophy of play have been carefully reviewed and reflected in the 3rd edition. Care was taken to maintain the *beginning* and *intermediate* skill level in the forefront of our consideration of the impact of the evolution of rules and strategy upon basic fundamentals.

Special thanks to Shawna Parrish, Jill Niles, Kurt Hanson, and the Men's Varsity Volleyball at California State University, Long Beach.

introduction

1

The evolution of volleyball in the United States has received a much needed boost since its adoption as an Olympic sport in 1964. Competitive programs in volleyball are now widespread and available for most age groups.

Volleyball is certainly one of the most popular participant sports in the U.S. today and world wide expansion of its popularity is clearly evident. Part of its popularity is due to the ease with which it can be modified to meet social and environmental restrictions, i.e., number of players on a side, court size, net height, etc. While these variations do not conform to all official rules, they are nonetheless exciting and fulfilling.

As skill in the sport improves, the participant becomes much more "rules" oriented and seeks out opportunities to become involved in competitive programs which are available for all levels of play. The impact of television, training films and clinics on "power" volleyball has led to an increasing appreciation for the fine points of the game. The improvement of equipment and instruction in the public school programs has also stimulated better progress at an earlier stage in the overall curriculum. Many secondary schools now have excellent competitive programs as a result of the skill development in prior programs.

The official rules call for six players on a team and the object of the game is to cause the ball to strike the floor on the opponent's court or to cause an opponent to engage in faulty play. A net, suspended across a 18m x 9m court, provides the playing area. Each team is arranged with three players across the front court near the net and three players behind them across the back court.

The game starts with the players facing the net and the right rear player of the team which won the toss stepping out of bounds behind the court into the 3m wide serving area. The server strikes the ball sharply causing it to fly over the net to the defensive team. The receiving team must then field the serve and return it over the net using no more than three hits. This pattern of three hits, not counting the hit off the block, is basic to the game. Ideally, the first hit is a pass to the center forward player, called the setter.

The setter then passes the ball into the air and parallel to the net so that one of the front flanking players can drive the ball into the opponent's court, preferably with such force that it cannot be returned before it hits the floor. If the receiving team is successful in returning the ball to the serving team, then the servers have three hits in which to put the ball back over the net. This exchanging is called a rally and continues until a team commits a fault or fails to return the ball over the net.

When a team wins the service all of its players rotate one position clockwise in order to bring a new server to the right rear corner. A team must hold its rotation order until the ball is served at which time rapid rearrangements enable players to move into advantageous positions. During this rearranging there can be some confusion since a back court player may move to the front court as a setter. This is legal, but the back court player, while in front of the 3m-line, may not block at the net or return the ball over the net if contact with the ball is above the net. All players must be in rotation order at the time of service. This ruling prevents one or two players from dominating the game. In coeducational play at least one of the three hits must be made by a girl for the same reason.

Points are scored only by the serving team and one point is awarded for each rally which is successful for the servers. If the receivers win the rally they then become the servers and are eligible to score points. A game is completed when a team scores 15 points or playing time has elapsed. A tie at 14-14, however, calls for additional play until one team succeeds in gaining a two point advantage. A match consists of a three out of five game series.

The sport of volleyball is well suited to today's living since it can be played and enjoyed by people of all ages. It also provides the opportunity to acquire a group of skills which can be used for many years in an almost injury free environment. At the same time it provides a highly competitive, action filled exercise pattern for large muscle groups. The level of competition and activity is regulated by the skill level of the players but it can be appropriately strenuous at all levels.

Most of us recognize that we feel better if we have regular, vigorous activity in which we can find relief from the tensions of work. Exercise contributes to the maintenance of muscle tone, helps control weight and provides much needed exercise for the heart muscle. For many years community programs have sponsored "noontimers" volleyball for businessmen. Here an individual has opportunity to relax in friendly, good-natured play with peers who are also seeking an outlet for their need for activity. During recent years the development of more adequate community recreation facilities has led to increasing numbers of evening volleyball periods for adults. These programs are usually co-recreational and so provide the married couple a chance to engage in a sport together. School programs have also recognized the growth of facilities and interest and are making an effort to prepare their students with sufficient skills to enable them to feel a sense of accomplishment while engaging in play.

At the beach the mobility of the game is well demonstrated. Two uprights, a net, a ball and 180' of rope (or lines scratched in the sand) provide a court which can be set up in 10 minutes. Many beaches, in fact, have courts or at least uprights in place throughout the year in order to meet the growing demands for recreational volleyball.

The following chapters will provide you with insight into the nature and requirements of this sport which brings pleasure and healthful exercise to so many people in the country.

HISTORY

Volleyball originated in the United States in 1895 and has gained such popularity through the world that it was included by the Japanese, as host country, in their 17 selections for the 1964 Olympic Games for both men and women. There have been considerable improvements in the two pieces of equipment necessary to play the game since it was first devised by William C. Morgan, a student at Springfield College and later director of the Holyoke, Massachusetts, YMCA. Prior to Morgan's graduation, he devised an idea for a new game which he called minonette. Borrowing skills from tennis, handball and baseball, he erected a tennis net at a height of 6'6" across the center of the gym. A rubber bladder from a basketball was used for the ball. Any number of players were allowed on each team and the object of the game was to hit or bat the ball back and forth over the net. The game was played in nine innings and each server had three outs before his team lost the ball.

Morgan took his game to his first job and introduced it to businessmen as a relaxing game, somewhat less strenuous than basketball. It was well received and in 1898 was reviewed, renamed "volleyball" and published in the proceedings of the Springfield College YMCA Sports Conference of that year.

Morgan also wrote the A.G. Spaulding & Bros. Company the specifications for a more suitable ball and there has been no appreciable change made in its design in the 80 years since that time. The official net used at this time is lighter than the tennis net and affords resiliency so that players can pick up a rebounding ball.

The YMCA instructors learned the game at Springfield but as they took it to the various YMCA's around the country they made modifications and revisions in the rules to accommodate special needs.

The original rules recorded in 1896 called for the game to be played in nine innings on a 25' x 50' court. The top of the net was supposed to be 6'6" off the ground and the ball 27" in circumference with a weight of nine to twelve ounces. The server stood with one foot on the back line and had two chances to bat the ball over the net. He was allowed assistance on his serve but no dribbling. A point could be scored only by the server. A net ball, after the first serve, or a line ball, was considered "out." Players could not touch the net or hold the ball and could dribble within only four feet of the net. A ball rebounding from any object outside the court was still in play.

In 1900 the YMCA brought volleyball to Canada, Central and South America and to the Orient, where it was not very popular for many years but is now widely played. In 1900 the YMCA Physical Directors Society adopted a new set of rules which eliminated the dribbling, first bounce and the innings. The game was now played to 21 points over a 7-foot net. The line ball was declared good and the ball could no longer be played off objects outside of the court.

Volleyball was introduced in Cuba in 1905, at the first annual convention of the Playgrounds of America Association (now the National Recreation Association) in 1907 and in Puerto Rico in 1909.

In 1912 the YMCA appointed a special committee to recommend rule changes. This committee moved the net higher, to 7'6", and made it 3 feet wide. The court was enlarged to 35' x 60' and a rule was devised for rotation of players. The serve could no longer touch the net and the two-game match was originated.

One rule which has remained virtually the same and which signifies the spirit of volleyball was recorded during the first YMCA Open Invitational Tournament held at Germantown, Pennsylvania, in 1912—the players called their own fouls. This annual tournament was held for the next ten years.

The evolution of the game for women proceeded in a slightly different direction. Women playing volleyball in YMCA programs and on amateur sport clubs played under the same rules as the men, except that the net height was placed at 7'4¼". However, volleyball played in schools and colleges was played under rules developed by the predecessor organization of the National Association for Girls and Women's Sports. (This association has had various names since its organization near the turn of the century, but has given continuous service in publishing rules for girls and women's sports.) The original rules allowed one player to assist the serve over the net, called for each team to be composed of nine players, each of whom was entitled to play to ball to herself before passing the ball to a teammate or over the net. During the mid-sixties various women's sport factions influenced NAGWS to revise its rules to bring them closer to those of USVBA. This transition is now complete with NAGWS and USVBA rules each publishing rules which are, in essence, identical.

Can you outline the historical development of volleyball by recalling: the name of the inventor? the original character of the game? the role of the YMCA in its development? the first date and place of inclusion in the Olympics? several of the organizations supporting and controlling the sport? the present status of volleyball?

The education profession recommended volleyball for all school and recreation programs in 1915 because its value as a team sport was realized, together with baseball, basketball and football. During the ten years that followed numerous rule changes were made. In 1917 the net was placed at eight feet and a game played to 15 points. The next year the six-man team was established. In 1921 the center line was put under the net and in 1922 the rule for hitting the ball only three times on each side was introduced. The court was made 30' x 60' in 1923 and it was decided that a team had to make two points in succession to win if the score reached 14-all. This rule was revised in 1925 to read that a team needed two points more than the other team in order to win if the score reached 14-all.

The evolution of the game to its present form for men was completed by 1925 and included the 8-foot net, six-man team, the marking of a center line, three hits on a side, 30' x 60' court and the 15-point game, with ties at 14-14 being settled by a two-point margin.

Volleyball is generally supported and controlled through the direction of the United States Volleyball Association (USVBA), American National Volleyball Association (ANVA), Association for Intercollegiate Athletics for Women (AIAW), National Collegiate Athletic Association (NCAA), National Association for Girl's and Women's Sports, Amateur Athletic Union (AAU), Young Men's Christian Association (YMCA), etc.

The United States Volleyball Association was organized in 1928 by Dr. George Fisher who is known as the "Father of Volleyball" and who from 1917 until his retirement in 1953 was the editor of the first Volleyball Guide published by the American Sports Publishing Co. of New York. The NCAA and the YMCA worked jointly with Dr. Fisher in editing the rules for the first Volleyball Guide which today serves to describe volleyball activities in all parts of the United States and which has been edited and published annually by the USVBA since the formation of that organization. A system for standardizing tournaments, qualifying officials and selecting representative teams has also been developed by the USVBA.

Volleyball as an international sport owes much of its prominence to the U.S. Armed Forces, which, as early as 1919, had distributed over 16,000 volleyballs to the American Expeditionary Forces and its allies (USVBA Guide, 1965). During World War II our servicemen carried the game all over the world. It is now played in more than 60 countries by more than 50 million people. It is the leading sport in 25 countries and ranks third internationally. The sport is especially popular in Japan and Europe. The first world's championship was held in Moscow's Dynamo Stadium in 1952. Julien Lenior,[2] then Secretary-Treasurer of the International Volleyball Federation which was formed in 1947, noted that 99 % of the 60,000 spectators understood the rules and appreciated the performance of the players in those games. The Federation, located in Paris, governs international rules and the annual world's volleyball championship. It is ironic than an American volleyball team has never won a world championship even though volleyball in this country has celebrated its seventieth anniversary. This curious fact is due, in part, to the development of a difference in rules and interpretation in European volleyball that has led to an advanced style of play which was difficult for Americans to accept. Recently, however, widespread acceptance of the international rules has created a new impetus for developing strong international caliber teams.

TERMINOLOGY

The enthusiasts in any sports area develop a jargon or specialized language to cover the specific skills and their applications in the games. Volleyball is no different and, although the jargon changes from one part of the country to another, the terms which are covered here are common to most places where volleyball is played extensively.

As the game opens, the six players on each team are arranged in rotation order with three front court and three back court players. Since this rotation order must be observed at the time of service, it is common to see a *switch* occur. This switch allows a temporary rearrangement of players after the serve for strategic purposes. Back court players who move ahead of the 3m line are restricted in terms of blocking and spiking. It is common for a spiker and setter in the front court to exchange positions so that the setter is between two spikers. From this position the setter can set the ball to either side. A *back-set* can be used to set the ball up to the spiker behind the setter. This skill is somewhat difficult to perform in a *clean* manner. This term refers to a ball's being distinctly hit, that is, it may not be carried, handled or *juggled* while it is in play. Examples of plays which are not clean are a *double*, or double hit, wherein the ball is played with one hand or touches another part of the body before it is contacted by the other hand, or a *throw* in which the player has a delayed contact with the ball. The development of a pair of clean hands takes a great deal of practice. Concern about consistent rulings on clean plays has led to the elimination of plays in which the open hand or hands are used to field the ball. Even though many beginners find it more simple to use open hands in an underhand motion to field low balls, it is illegal to use this

Fig. 1.1   A clean recovery

technique. It is much better to learn to pass or dig the ball as described in the skills section of this book.

During play it is not uncommon to hear words with special meanings. Occasionally a spiker, seeing that he is confronted by a good block, will *dink* the ball. The dink is a light tap that drops the ball just over and behind the block. It is for this reason that one player is usually assigned to *cover* the block, meaning that he must be prapared to move into the area behind the block to field the "dink."

If a spiker runs too far under a set he may change his hitting style to a *roundhouse*. In this maneuver the spiker swings a straight arm in an arc until he contacts the ball, thus imparting a topspin to the ball with a good deal of force. It is effective as change of pace and will sometimes be used as a serving technique as well.

The spiker can also hit either *off hand* or *on hand* depending on whether the ball crosses in front of the body before it is hit. *On hand* means the ball is contacted before it crosses in front of the body.

Contributions to playing techniques have been developed internationally. The *spike*, for example, is reputed to have been introduced by a little-known team in a tournament in Manila.[3] This "backwoods" team had the habit of

Fig. 1.2   Spiking action

passing the ball high in the air so that a large, rangy bushman could run in and hit it. The opposing teams had no defense for this maneuver and, since it did not violate any existing rules, it has developed into a highly-skilled art, the practice of which makes the game an exciting spectator as well as participant sport. Dr. Charles McCloy, a researcher from the University of Iowa, published material stating that a volleyball spike travels an average of 62 m.p.h. with exceptional shots attaining speeds of 110 m.p.h. Spikes traveling nearly 100 feet per second require a high degree of defensive skill and quick action if they are to be recovered.

Has the change to metric measurement increased or decreased the overall size of an official court? Why do you think the metric measurements have been adopted?

A *multiple offense* is when a back court player becomes the *setter* and thus enabling all three front court players to become potential spikers. The setter may use a variety of sets including a *shoot* set in which the ball is directed in a straight line to the spikers position or a *short* set in which the spiker leaps in the air and waits for set to rise just above the net before it is struck. These variations permit deception to be introduced into the game.

To field the hard hit spike requires the player to develop skill in the use of the *dig*. This term refers to any action to play the hard spike, whether it is a well-executed *pass* or a desperation effort to simply rebound the ball up into the air with any part of the fist, hand, or arm so that the ball is maintained *in play*.

The *dive* is often utilized to bring the player into a position to "dig" the ball. This skill can be executed in either of two ways. In the first, the player drives head long in a path parallel to the floor surface, extending one or both arms under the ball to rebound the ball upward. The second technique, developed by the Japanese, involves a sideward or forward lunge toward the ball, pivoting to the thigh and hip as the ball is fielded, followed by a *shoulder roll* to bring the player quickly back to the feet.

Many innovations have also been developed as a result of the refinements in the game as it is played on the beaches, particularly in Southern California. The court dimensions are regulation but only two players are available to cover this space. In recent years, two-man women's play has improved to the point where the play is nearly as fast and aggressive as the game played by the males. This type of play has, in fact, been instrumental in the revision of women's rules until they have become identical except for net height to the men's.

One of the areas of great weakness in volleyball in the United States, however, centers in the school framework. Even though the game is widely played and widely taught, the technique for higher levels of play have frequently been neglected. This is usually due to a lack of understanding on the part of the teacher who finds the game easy to control and teach to the point where everyone enjoys it. The progress in skill development at this point is dependent upon stressing "clean" ball handling and adherence to the rules concerning play at the net. "Throwing" the ball can be perfected to the point where a player who *might* become a good, "clean" player is reluctant to discard the skills which make him effective in a loosely played game. This lack of attention to progressive development in play unfortunately results in relatively little improvement during the junior and senior high school days.

the game

2

Rules governing play in volleyball have evolved steadily since the origination of the game. During the early development, rules varied considerably with the needs of various organizations who promoted competition. Confusion which resulted led to a major attempt at universality in the United States and was followed very shortly by adoption of the International rules for play in U.S. competition. It is anticipated that International rules will supercede all others.

THE COURT

The volleyball court recently changed into metric measurements has a playing surface which is 18 meters (59') long and 9 meters (29'6") wide with a ceiling clearance of 7 meters (23'). The court is bounded by 5 cm (2") wide lines which are included into the playing area. It is important to place the court so that a minimum of 2 meters (6'6") of clearance is kept around the court. The court is divided by three lines across the width. One center line and two attack lines which parallel the center line at a distance of 3 meters (9'10"). The attack lines are 5 cm (2") wide and are included in the attack area.

There should also be a marked service area 3 meters (9'10") wide at the right rear corner of the court. This area should be 2 meters (6'6") deep and should be marked on the right and left sides by a 15 cm (6") line, 5 cm (2") wide that is begun 20 cm (8") behind the end line of the court.

It should be noted that many of these metric dimensions vary slightly from the courts which have been laid out in feet and inches.

A special heavy duty net measuring 1 meter (3'3") wide and 9.5 meters (32') long with 10 cm (4") wide square mesh is tautly stretched from all four corners across the court over the center line. Turnbuckles are commonly used to tighten the top rope or wire cable of the net. The height of the net is 2.43 meters (7'11⅝") for men and 2.24 meters (7'4⅛") for women. This height may be only 2 cm (¾") higher at the side edges of the net.

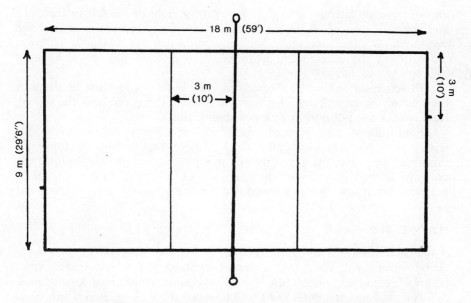

Fig. 2.1   Volleyball court

Antennae are to be placed on the net directly above the side line on each end of the net. Any ball crossing the net which touches the antennae is considered to be out of bounds. Weak or sagging nets dramatically change the quality of the game.

THE BALL

The volleyball itself has evolved until a laceless sphere made of leather or the equipment is available with a circumference of 65-67 cm (25¾-26¼") and at least twelve panels. This ball, which is to weigh 260-280 grams (9-10 oz.), should be inflated to a pressure between .48 and .52 kg/cm. This standardization has been an important factor in developing effective service and passing techniques. Lists of approved volleyballs can be found in the USVBA Guide which contains official rules and regulations for the sport. Synthetic or rubber balls have generally been less desirable since they tend to be heavier and more slippery than their leather counterparts.

Teams, Players, Positions and Substitutes

A volleyball *team* consists of six players positioned into a front line and a back line of three players each. At the time the ball is contacted on the service all players shall be positioned in serving order, and each front line player must be totally in front of each of his respective backline players so that their feet in no way overlap. At the same time each player in both front and back line may not overlap laterally with the player to the right or the left in the same line. After the service all players may move to play or cover any area of the court with the stipulation that a back line player may not return the ball over the net from above net height while in advance of the ten foot line, and a back row player may not block.

Players must follow the *serving order* established with their positions at the start of the game. After the loss of service by the opponents, the serving team rotates one position in a clockwise direction.

Substitutions may be made upon request of and recognition by the referee or umpire when the ball is dead. A player may reenter the game one time providing that the player is in the same rotation position which was occupied during the previous entry. Each team is limited to 6 substitutions per game. Each team is also allowed two time outs for rest during each game.

PLAYING THE GAME

A *match* consists of five games. The team winning 3 out of 5 games is declared the winner. The *game* is played until one team has scored fifteen points. The winning team must lead by two points before play is concluded.

A *toss of the coin* determines which team will serve first and which court each team will occupy, the choice being given the winner of the toss and the loser receiving the alternate choice. Teams *change courts* after each game and at eight points into the 5th game. The team not serving first in the first game serves first in the second game, and so on.

Two minutes are taken between games for rest and reorganization. Each team is permitted to call two team time-outs per game, the length of the time-out being thirty seconds.

The game is started with a service by the right back player on the serving team. The server is permitted to put the ball into play on each serve only after the referee has sounded his whistle. The player must be outside the court and within the service area until the ball is contacted on the serve. The ball may be hit or batted with the hand, fist, or arm, after being thrown into the air and is directed over the net between the side lines into the opponents' court. The server continues until his team loses the service or the game is completed. When one team loses the service its opponents will serve after having rotated one position clockwise. During the service it is illegal for a team to screen the server's action from the opponents' view in any way. If this occurs, side-out is called. It is also illegal to serve out of order. If the error is discovered during the service, all points scored during that service are deducted and the service is terminated. If, however, the error is not discovered until after the opponents have served after the illegal order, no penalty is assessed, but positions must be corrected.

After the service the ball must be *clearly hit* when it is volleyed by any player. It may be contacted with any part of the body above (and including) the waist, as long as a player does not play the ball twice in succession. If the ball contacts two parts of the body at the same time, this is considered to be one play. Simultaneous contact of the ball by teammates or by two opponents (above the net) constitutes one play, and either player may play the ball again.

In addition, if a player participating in a block contacts the ball, he may play it again. Each team may play the ball only three times before it crosses the net to the opponents' court. Hits on the block do not count as one of the three hits. A player may go outside the court to play the ball, provided that any ball hit over the net from out of bounds must cross the net over or between the sidelines.

When *playing at the net*, a player may not touch the net or its cable while the ball is in play. A player returning the ball may reach over the net to follow any otherwise legal play, as long as he first contacts the ball on his own side of the net. It is legal to reach over the net to block an opponent's hit, provided the opponent has hit the ball to return it. The ball may be played off the net. It is legal to touch the center line but illegal to touch beyond it into the opponents' court. It is also legal for a player to reach under the net to play a ball which is in play on his court, but it is illegal to reach under the net and interfere with opponents' activity.

CONDUCT

The team captain is the only player in the game who can speak to the officials.

FOULS AND PENALTIES

A *foul* is an infraction of the rules or a failure to play the ball properly. The penalty for fouls is a point scored for the opponents if the foul is committed by the receiving team, or side-out (loss of service) if the foul is committed by the serving team.

Fouls are called whenever (1) the server is out of the service area before the ball is contacted; (2) any player is illegally positioned on the service; (3) screening of the service is used; (4) a backline player, in attempting to spike, goes into the air in front of the attack line; (5) a player serves out of order; (6) the server fails to hit the ball clearly with hand, fist or arm; (7) the server hits the ball out of bounds, into the net, or fails to hit it completely over the net; (8) a player causes the ball to land out of bounds at any time during the play; (9) a player does not clearly hit the ball (the ball may not visibly come to rest at the time it is contacted by the player); (10) one plays the ball successively (exception: after participating in a block or after having made a simultaneous hit with either a teammate or an opponent, a player may play the ball again); (11) a team plays the ball more than three times before sending it to the opponents' court, the contact of the ball by the block is not counted as one of the three hits; (12) a substitute returns to the game in a position other than his original one, in relation to his teammates; (13) a server unnecessarily delays putting the ball into play; (14) a player touches the net, reaches over the net, crosses the center line, or interferes with opponents under the net while the ball is in play (exception: a blocker may reach over the net to block a return provided the opponent has hit the ball; (15) a starting player re-enters the game more than one time or a substitute re-enters; (16) a player delays the game in any unnecessary manner; (17) a team calls more than two time-outs per game.

If unsportsmanlike conduct occurs, the official may warn the player or invoke the penalty for the foul. For repetition the official may disqualify the player from the game.

If two opponents commit fouls simultaneously, a double foul is called and the point is replayed.

Several other violations of rules may occur during play. These are summarized as follows: (1) a time-out is charged to a team which fails to substitute without delay; (2) a player entering the game for the third time (or second time for a substitute) or in the wrong position must leave the game; (3) all points scored are cancelled if made by an improper server or while an illegally entered or positioned re-entry player is on the court. (4) a forfeit game, scoring 15-0, is called if a team does not have six players or refuses to begin play.

A *point is replayed* whenever (1) an official commits an error; (2) any object enters the court or there is interference with play; (3) a player serves the ball before the official's whistle signals for service; (4) a player is injured and a time-out is called while the ball is in play; (5) a double foul occurs.

COEDUCATIONAL RULES

All rules given above apply to coeducational play except: (1) the serving order shall alternate one man and one woman throughout the line-up (2) when the ball is played by more than one player on a side, one hit shall be made by a woman before the ball is returned to the opponents; (3) the net shall be 2.43 m (7'11⅝" in height); and (4) when one male player is in the front row one back row player may come to the net to block.

DOUBLES RULES

All rules given above apply to doubles play except: (1) each team's court measure thirty feet wide and twenty-five feet deep; (2) no substitutes are permitted; (the serve must come from the right half of the rear court area; (4) a game consists of eleven points or five minutes actual playing time.

BEACH RULES

All rules given prior to the foregoing sections apply except (1) the net is placed seven feet and ten inches above hard packed sand, and seven feet and nine inches above loosely packed sand; (2) teams change courts after each five points are scored; (3) ropes are used as boundaries; (4) contact with the center rope is a foul, but if a player's foot is under the rope without contacting it, no foul is called.

Fig. 2.2   Beach volleyball

OFFICIALS AND THEIR DUTIES

For the purpose of controlling play in a manner equitable to each team, the following officials are used: a referee, an umpire, a timekeeper, a scorekeeper, and two to four linesmen.

The *referee*, the official in charge, is stationed in an elevated position at one end of the net and makes decisions on all playing of the ball, declares point and side-out, and may at anytime overrule another official if he feels an error has occurred. The referee shall confer with and instruct all the other officials with reference to their duties. The referee indicates that play shall start on each service with a whistle. The whistle is blown to indicate that any infraction of the rules has occurred during play. The referee should use appropriate signals to indicate his calls. *Signals* include: (1) point—hand nearest team scoring raised with forefinger extended; (2) side-out—hand nearest team to gain the service is extended toward that team with hand open, palm upward; (3) over the net—hand extended over the net from side of the infraction; (4) touching the net—touch the net on the side of the infraction; (5) line foul—hand extended toward the line on the side of the infraction; (6) held ball—underhand lifting motion upward; (7) time-out—hands form a T on side of team requesting time-out; (8) substitution—hands are rotated around one another in front of body.

The umpire, stationed at the opposite end of the net from the referee, assists in calling violations regarding positioning, conduct, substitution, and interference with play, as well as makes decisions in regard to net and center line fouls. The umpire uses the same signals as the referee whenever appropriate. He also keeps time on time outs.

The scorer, seated near the umpire's position, is charged with keeping an accurate account of the score and all other recorded information, and informing the referee or umpire of violations or fouls committed by either team relative to substitution, positioning, or time-outs.

Linesmen are positioned at the rear corners of the court to assist in indicating whether balls are in or out of court. The linesman should have a small flag in hand, indicating "out" by raising the hand with flag, and indicating "in" by pointing the flag downward. Linesmen also assist in watching to see that the server remains in the serving area and that a ball crossing the net from out of bounds crosses between the net markers for the sideline. They also assist in retrieving the ball when time-outs are called. If two linesmen are used, each is positioned at the left rear corners and is responsible for the rear court line and the sideline on his side of the court. If four linesmen are used, the rear court linesmen are positioned on the right rear corners, and the side linesmen are positioned on the left rear court corners.

basic skills

3

The game of volleyball, when properly played, requires that the participants make specific adaptations to the artificial environment and value system of the game. This requirement is often overlooked by beginners who rarely identify the problems whose solutions lead to increased efficiency and effectiveness in play.

The dimensions of the courts (18m x 9m) and the barrier (2.24m for women and 2.43m for men) indicate that short, quick movements and jumping are critical skills which are required in order to adapt to the physical limitations of the court. The light, well inflated ball necessitates the development of ball handling skills which result in a high degree of control both in direction and magnitude.

Moving quickly on the court depends upon adequate strength and endurance coupled with alertness. The strength and endurance requirements are quite specific and should be met through drills or game situations that involve the body in the exact movement roles appropriate to the game and with ever increasing work demands. If there are adequate levels of strength and endurance, the readiness of the individual becomes the critical element. Too often players stand erect, hands at their sides, waiting for the ball. When it comes they must raise their hands and arms, bend at the knees and then start to move. Logically the time taken to prepare to move is wasted, since the preparation could have been incorporated into the waiting stance. The "ready" position for volleyball is one in which the knees are slightly bent, hands are carried about waist height, the body is balanced and attention is focused on the ball.

Jumping in volleyball is usually performed near the net. This means that the jumping style must be adapted to keep the player from touching the net. The tendency to jump forward results in fouls. It is important, therefore, to learn that you must move to the place where you wish to jump and then transfer essentially all of your momentum so that it goes up parallel to the net. Beginning players who jump and fly through the air become a hazard to teammates and a help to opponents.

Fig. 3.1   The ready position

Ball handling skills are probably the most critical skills to be developed since the circumstances for their application change very rapidly during play.

Can you place 10 consecutive underhand serves in the rear one-third of the opponent's court? Can you equal your underhand performance with the overhand serve?

THE SERVE

The serve is extremely important because only by retaining the service can a team score points. It is necessary to do more than just get the ball over the net. Each player on the team should be able to place a serve accurately anywhere in the opponent's court. Any time you can put the opponents on the defensive with your serve, you are that much closer to winning the game.

The first consideration when serving is to be aware of body position. The server must remain in the 3m service area and may not step on a boundary line of that area. Avoiding service faults is of prime importance, and the best remedy for hitting a ball into the net, ceiling or out-of-bounds is purposeful practice. Thinking through the entire serve, taking a deep breath, exhaling half of it and relaxing before executing the movement take just a few seconds and should result in a good serve accurately placed.

The Overhand Serve—This serve is used by the majority of leading players because it can be placed accurately and if delivered correctly will

Fig. 3.2 The overhand serve

"float" or wobble, putting the opponent on the defensive because he will have to make a quick adjustment to receive the ball. It often causes the receiver to make either an off-center or illegal pass.

The right-handed server stands facing the net with the left foot slightly forward. The ball is tossed with both hands, to prevent it from spinning, to a height .7-1m above the head and about .5m forward of the shoulder. The right arm is brought back and the wrist and elbow cocked. As the elbow leads the way, it is extended so that the player is reaching with a fairly straight arm as the ball is contacted solidly with the heel of the hand. If the ball is tossed too far forward the hand contacts it above the center line of the ball and it probably will not clear the net. On the other hand if the ball is tossed too close to the head it will be punched to the ceiling or perhaps hit out of bounds. It is important to hit behind and slightly below the center of the mass of the ball to avoid sending it out of bounds to either sideline. To make the ball float and drop it is necessary to keep it from spinning during delivery. To accomplish this the ball is struck sharply with no wrist action after contact. Contacting the ball in line with the upper arrow in figure 3.3 will cause a downward flight—a net serve. Contacting the ball in line with the lower arrow will usually result in a serve which skims the net and is difficult to field.

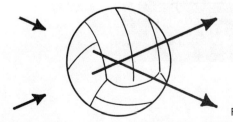

Fig. 3.3 Result of contact upon ball flight

The Underhand Serve—This is a good consistent method for getting the ball over the net; however, it does not have the effect of the overhand serve because it is generally not difficult for the defense to receive and pass. It is easy to learn to place the underhand serve but seldom does it put your opponents on the defensive.

Stand facing the net, knees bent, with the left foot forward and the left arm extended across the front of the body. The ball rests on the palm of the left hand. The right arm is swung straight back, then forward to strike the ball with the heel of the hand or the flat fist (palm forward). The head should be bent slightly forward as this helps to keep the ball lower so it will skim the net. As the ball is struck you step forward with your right foot as you follow through with the swing of your right arm. Again it is important to contact the ball solidly and directly at the point which will result in a proper trajectory.

Fig. 3.4 The underhand serve

THE FOREARM PASS

The forearm pass is the technique used to field serves and spikes. Successful team play is dependent upon the effective performance of the forearm pass, since it is usually made as the first hit on a team's side of the net and must be executed with control and accuracy in order for the set and the spike to occur.

Place a line 1m long at a height of 1.7m on a smooth wall. Standing 1m from the wall, can you volley 10 consecutive forearm passes above the line? 15? 20?

The forearm pass requires that the ball strike both forearms simultaneously and be directed high into the air toward the setter who will in turn position the ball for the spiker. This pass, shown in figure 3.5, is aptly named since the ball rebounds from the flat surface which is placed in its path. Swinging the arms to meet the ball will result in an unnecessarily high pass which can hit the ceiling or travel out of bounds.

Fig. 3.5   The forearm pass

To get into position for the forearm pass the player must move quickly to a position in line with the flight of the ball. Too often the novice reaches for the ball and then attempts to move to it. A better technique is to move the body first and then do whatever minor arm positioning is necessary to achieve an accurate well controlled pass. *Run and reach, don't reach and run.*

Once the body is in position the forearms are brought together with the thumbs parallel and the fingers of one hand in the palm of the other hand. This placement will result in a relatively flat surface for rebound should the ball be misjudged. The angle of the forearm will in a large measure dictate the angle of the return flight of the ball. If the forearms are perpendicular to the path of the incoming ball it should rebound exactly away in the path from which it came. Thus the angles of incidence and reflection become critical to controlling the ball. Bending the elbows sharply will often cause the ball to fly back over the head. This is usually undesirable except when it is necessary to play the ball back over the head to save it.

Since the forearm pass is often used to play a hard hit spike or serve, several factors in balance of the body are important to control of the force and direction of the resulting pass.

The stance used is a combination of the forward-back and the side-stride position. From this stance the player will be able to move quickly in order to adjust any sudden changes in the flight of the ball. The ankles, knees and hips should be flexed into a comfortable semi-crouch position. From this position the player can absorb the force of hard hits by giving with the hit by shifting the weight backward over the stance as the hit is played. In addition, the stance allows the player to add force to soft hits by extending the legs. The arms should never be swung upward to produce force. Rather, the legs are extended so that the forearm surface can remain at a constant angle throughout the play. There is a slight lifting of the shoulders in the follow-through of the pass.

It is desirable to position so that the ball is played on the midline of the body. If the ball comes to the player outside the midline area, it is necessary to move the feet to get in a position behind the ball.

If the ball is received from one direction and the desired pass is in another direction, it is necessary to move to a position so the entire body faces the desired direction of the pass.

From a position under the ball, how would the setter move to set up the player behind him? Which foot should be moved to set up a player to the right?

In case the ball is so far out of reach to the player's right or left that it is not possible to move quickly enough to get directly behind the ball, it is desirable to make the following adjustment. Plant the foot nearest the ball and pivot with that foot toward the direction of the path desired for the pass, rotating the ball toward the target with the arms in the same stable position described above.

A less frequently used variation is the one arm pass or "dig" which is used as a desperation measure when the ball is nearly out of reach. This pass is difficult to control and should not be used as a preferred technique. It requires much more practice and is considered an advanced skill.

Considerable practice is necessary before a player learns appropriate positioning of the forearms for reaching to the sides, over the head and for very low balls. The frustrations in learning the skills are, however, usually forgotten in the satisfactions which come as a result of accomplishment of the technique.

The Net Recovery—If the ball is hit into the net on the first or second contact it is possible to keep it in play if it can be bounced into the air again. The forearm pass or the dig is used for this recovery shot. When it is performed correctly it looks easy and smooth. The most important consideration in this shot is watching where the ball strikes the net. A ball landing near the top of the net will drop almost straight down. If it hits the center of the net it will rebound out .3-.7m before dropping. A ball that contacts near the bottom of the net will most often be held by the net momentarily before rolling out and down.

Fig. 3.6   Net recovery

The player watches the ball and with experience and practice can determine where to position himself for its recovery. He turns his side to the net and crouches in order to contact the ball as close to the floor as possible. If it is to be the second hit the player should try to bounce the ball up and back to avoid hitting it back into the net. This also gives his teammates a better opportunity to spike or place the ball on the third hit. If it is to be the third contact with the ball, the player attempts to hit it up and over the net. This particular shot is difficult to achieve but can be done with practice.

THE SET

This skill is used to take a pass and alter its flight so that the ball will be put into the air at a location where the spiker can drive it down onto the opponent's court. It is possibly the most critical portion of the pass-set-spike pattern since it depends upon precise execution for an accurate set to the spiker. The cardinal rule for the setter is *to get into position under the ball.* The

Fig. 3.7   The set

head is up, looking at the ball, the elbows are out, the hands are up, the knees are bent and one foot is slightly advanced. See figure 3.7.

The fingers are cupped slightly so that the fingers and thumbs contact the ball at the same time. The ball *never* touches the palms of the hands during the set. The wrists are laid back with the palms facing upward. Index fingers and thumbs should form a triangular window that the setter can look through to see the incoming ball. The tips of the thumbs are about 15cm apart. Setting involves the whole body and as the ball is contacted the ankles, knees, hips, shoulders, elbows and wrists each provide a portion of the effort that is expended on the ball. Recall that a "clean" set cannot be made easily if the elbows are kept close to the body, so keep the elbows comfortable to the outside.

The ball is most easily set in the direction the body is facing and therefore body position is of prime importance. If the setter is under the ball some alternative moves are possible. By taking a slight step back just before the ball is contacted he can set up the spiker he faces. If he takes a step forward he can easily set up the player behind him. The setter should delay taking this step until the last second in order to keep the opponent blockers unaware of who will be receiving the ball. The setter places the ball between 45-60cm from the net and at least 1.7m above the net. As in the pass, the ball should arch, hang and then drop directly in the position desired. Through the use of signals the setter can let his spikers know to whom he is giving the ball and where they will receive it. By setting up the ball at either corner of the net it is easier to spread out the blockers on the opponent's team. At advanced

Fig. 3.8   Hand position for the overhead pass

levels of play the setter may set . . . "short" sets, which are lower and thus require a faster response and "shoot" sets, which are rapid, line of sight passes out to a spiker at the side of the net. These advanced skills can be used to confuse the opponents blocking maneuvers but they carry a greater risk of failure and require a great deal of practice and coordination between the setter and the spiker.

Even though the setter does not receive a perfect pass from the back line and it is necessary for him to move under the ball he should be able to set up his spikers for the kill. The second ball always goes to the front set unless he calls for help from another player.

The setter should know his spikers' capabilities and know where they like the ball placed. With purposeful practice, teamwork will evolve that permits the players to use numerous variations of the set and thus improve their effectiveness.

THE SPIKE

The spike constitutes one of the most difficult to coordinate acts found in any sport. The player must be able to run, jump high, time a moving ball, hit it solidly, and at the same time try to place it in a certain spot. Additionally, the spiker must land and immediately become a "ready" defensive player. It is a spectacular skill to observe and even more spectacular to perform.

Stand 4-5m from a smooth wall. Using a spiking action, hit the ball downward so that it strikes the floor 1-1.7m from the wall and rebounds against the wall and back into the air toward you. Can you execute another spike off of the rebound? Can you do 5 successive spikes? 8? 10?

Fig. 3.9   The spike

The spike is varied by almost every player to his individual preference; however, a great deal of study has been made of this skill and there are certain actions which must be performed to accomplish a hard, fast drive on the ball.

The potential spiker is usually located away from the net during the time the ball is being passed. As the setter gains control, the spiker is moving toward the net and gaining momentum. As the set goes up, the spiker transfers the forward momentum into upward momentum by utilizing a two foot take off near the net. The spiker should time the take off so that the upward momentum will carry the body upward, not forward.

The run is made from 3-4m back and varies among players from a long stride to short steps or a glide. The crouching position is assumed in order to give more impetus to the jump. The jump is made approximately .6-1m behind the ball so it is above the head and about 30cm in front of the spiking shoulder. The player does not come up under the ball. As he jumps both arms are swung upward and the upper trunk is rotated to the right with the left shoulder toward the net. The left arm is carried higher for balance. As the left arm is driven down, the shoulders become parallel to the net. The elbow leads as the spiking arm whips forward and it acts as a pivot to prevent the arm from hitting the net. The arm straightens as the wrist snaps forward to drive the heel of the hand into the ball. With enough height to the jump, the ball can be hit with the heel of the open hand as the hand and fingers are snapped forward. The ball is directed over the net and down into the court.

The player must be prepared for his spiked ball to be blocked, in which case it would drive right back down at him. He must also be balanced to prevent falling into the net or over the center line. The defense for these problems is handled in the follow-through. The player lands with knees bent and elbows close to the body for balance and with hands ready for a quick dig on a blocked ball.

Even if the ball is set up too far back from the net for the conventional spike, it still can be attacked in much the same manner. The ball is contacted slightly behind the vertical line of shoulder with the heel of the hand. The fingers are held rigid and the heel of the hand strikes sharply upward, across the rear of the ball, thus imparting top spin. The top spin causes the ball to drop in a sharper arc.

Common faults in spiking are hitting the ball out of bounds or into the net. These faults can be remedied with the development of proper timing, a sufficiently high jump, and proper position of the hand as contact is made with the ball. Timing is critical since hitting the ball during its ascent will tend to result in hitting under the center of mass of the ball. This will result in a trajectory which will carry the ball out of bounds. Hitting the ball too late during its descent can result in a net or missed ball as a result of hitting on top of the ball. Proper timing will permit the ball to be struck as it appears to "hang" during the period when the ball is changing direction from ascent to descent or during the early stages of dropping while the ball is still well above the net. The ball should be struck with the heel of the hand, fingers carrying over the upper part of the ball, with the ball .3-.6m in front of the shoulder of the spiking arm. Striking at the ball with the fist will often result in a wild hit since the timing becomes even more critical.

A common fault in jumping for the spike is leaving the ground too soon. One must learn to time the jump so that you reach your maximum height at a time when the ball is just beginning its drop. Jumping too early will result in the predicament where the ball continues to move away from the spiker and stays just out of reach during ascent as well as descent. Approaching too soon will result in the spiker stopping to wait for the ball to descend to hitting position and therefore losing the momentum of the approach into the jump for the spike.

basic strategy
4

Team play is *essential* in volleyball. The effectiveness of any team is directly related to the coordination of the abilities and responsibilities of its members. Outstanding spiking does not occur without precision setting. The setter's ability to place the ball for the spiker depends largely upon the ability of the team's members to control the ball on the first volley as it comes from the opponents' court. The possibility of controlling the first hit is dependent upon a well coordinated defense. Each player must do his best to enhance the team's play.

Each game situation places new and different demands upon each player in each position on the court. Successful teamwork requires that a player know all the team patterns which have been established, think quickly and anticipate situations before they arise, and make a maximum effort to carry out his responsibilities.

Mark a 1m x 1m square 60cm from the net midway between the sidelines. With a partner tossing for you, can you pass the ball from the right back position to a height of 3-5m so that it lands on the marker? Can you do it from the center and left back positions? Can you do five successive hits from each?

The sections which follow are designed to present concepts of offense and defense in volleyball. The first section, *Basic Concepts of Strategy and Team Play*, covers the fundamentals of team play which the beginning player and team should follow, and upon which most intermediate and advanced strategy concepts are based. The second section, *Intermediate Offensive and Defensive Concepts*, cover these aspects in depth and should be useful for players and teams who have begun to master the fundamental techniques of the game. *Advanced Offensive and Defensive Concepts* are briefly surveyed in section three to acquaint the reader with the potential of strategy for the game of volleyball. The final section is devoted to some approaches to strategy in *Coeducational Volleyball*.

BASIC CONCEPTS OF STRATEGY AND TEAM PLAY

Basic Pass Pattern. The spike is the key offensive weapon in volleyball. To insure opportunities for the spike, a general pass pattern is used. As the ball comes over the net from the opponents' court, whether on a serve, a rally return or off a block, an attempt should be made to *pass* (1) the ball to the setter, usually the center front player. The setter then *sets* (2) the ball to either the left front or right front player for the spike (3). The *pass-set-spike* pattern is the basis for volleyball offense. (Figure 4.1)

The right and left front positions are considered to be the fundamental spiker's positions because the distances to the farthest boundaries of the opponents' court are generally longer from these positions than from the center front. This affords a spiker a choice of angles for the spike with the assurance of the greatest possibility of keeping the ball within the court boundaries. Figure 4.2 illustrates these angles with solid line arrows. The center spiking angles are shown in figure 4.2 with dotted line arrows. It can be readily seen that angles available to the center spiker result in generally shorter distances than those available to the left or right front spiker. The center hit is a planned strategy at advanced levels of play when spikers have the skill capabilities of placing the spike with the high degree of accuracy demanded.

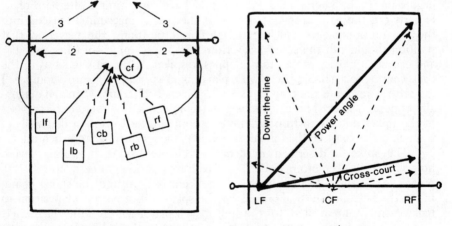

Fig. 4.1   Pass-set-spike pattern   Fig. 4.2   Hitting angles

Assuming that all the spikers on a team are right handed, the left front position is known as the *on-hand* spiking position. This term is used because the spiker's hitting arm is on the same side as the direction of the approaching set. Conversely, the right front position is called the *off-hand* side because the set must cross the spiker's body to be in position for the spiking hand. For lefthanded spikers the left front position is the off-hand, and the right front position is the on-hand side.

The first hit on the side, or the *pass*, is normally executed with the forearm pass. The pass should be directed toward the center front area of the court to a height of about 1.5-2.5m above net height. This height of arc is necessary to give the setter time to get into position to make a good set. The pass should be placed in front of the setter as the setter faces the sideline. This is preferred to a pass directly overhead or behind the setter so that the setter is able to move forward to execute the play.

The *set* should be placed in a position from which the spiker can attack the ball. A regular set is placed 50-70cm from the net and about 1.5m above net height. The set should be placed wide, toward the sideline, so that the spiker will approach the ball from slightly outside the court and contact the ball just inside the sideline. Wide sets are desirable since this allows longer spiking angles, and forces the defense to cover the full 9 meter width of the court and net.

The setter must move quickly to the pass and should make every attempt to squarely face the direction of the desired set. The setter should feel obligated to get to the ball if the pass is placed anywhere near the center front of the court. He should attempt to move constantly with one side to the net rather than turning his back to the net to watch the passer. With his side to the net the setter can turn the head to watch the ball and sliding steps can be taken to the ball while facing the direction of the desired set. Moving to the ball with the back to the net forces the setter to accomplish between a 90 and 180 degree turn to face the position for the set.

Inaccurate passing occurs at all levels of play, but happens most often at beginning levels. Therefore, a team should have some simple alternate plans to carry out the pass-set-spike patterns. If the pass is inaccurately placed into the air and approaches the left or right front positions, the player in that position should call the setter away from the play ("mine" or "I've got it") and execute a *cross-court set* to the opposite spiker. If the pass remains in the back court, the available back court player who is facing forward should call the setter away from the play and should place a *back-court set* to the diagonally opposite spiker. The diagonal set is recommended in preference to a set to the spiker directly in front of the back-court player because a diagonal set is much easier to spike than a ball which approaches directly from behind.

The *spike* is described in detail in chapter 3. At beginning levels, however, the spiker often finds it difficult to position properly for the approach to the spike. Often a pass and set occur only to find the spiker standing at the net, unable to approach for the spike and often out of position to make even a jump in place for the spike. Each player who is either in the left or right front position must *think like a spiker*. As the ball is passed on the first hit, if the spiker is not needed to assist as a setter, he should retreat immediately to about 3m from the net and on or outside the sideline to await the set. If the pass comes between the spiker and the setter, the spiker should let the setter take it so that the spiker can be available to spike. If the ball comes over the net in such a way that either setter or spiker could make the pass (first hit), the spiker should take the ball and pass to the setter who will in turn set for the spiker.

It is often necessary to *play an inaccurate set* over the net. There are several alternatives when the set is so off-target that the spike is not possible. The one hand top-spin hit can be used if the player is able to face the net behind the ball to hit the ball overhead. This is a spike-type hitting action which places the ball to deep court areas with a good deal of force. The player positions himself so that the ball is at full arm's reach overhead and 25-35cm in front of the hitting shoulder. By hitting from below the center of gravity of the ball with sharp upward pressure the desired top-spin is gained. The farther the ball is from the net, the lower on the ball is the contact point required to gain the proper trajectory for the ball to cross the net.

If the pass and set are so poorly controlled that the third hit will be played from out of bounds, from deep court, or from an off-balance position, the forearm pass should be used to play the ball over the net. The basic objective is to get the ball over the net and to keep the ball in play. The player making this play should turn the side to the net, take a wide stride position, drawing the arms (positioned for the forearm pass) back with the rear arm and shoulder higher than the forward arm and shoulder. The ball is stroked with the forward motion of the arms and a forceful weight shift to the forward foot. The side to the net position is recommended in preference to a back to the net position so that the player can have a better perspective of the angle and flight needed to place the ball over the net into the opponents' court.

Receiving Service. The server who can place the serve or who can create deceptive floating or spinning action of the ball is on the offensive. This makes the receiving of the service a defensive maneuver. The serve must be handled and controlled before the receiving team can assume the offensive. Careful observation by experienced teams and coaches has indicated that the majority of serves in most volleyball games fall into the middle third of the receiving team's court. For good coverage, then, the receiving team should flood this center court area with each player aware of the area for which he has responsibility. If the individual server serves consistently deep or short the entire team alignment can make minor adjustments to cover these circumstances.

Figure 4.3 shows the recommended alignment for receiving service. The center front player is near the net to be out of the receiving formation and to be available to make the set. The setter is off-set to the right so that any one of the receiving players can more easily pass the ball in front of the setter as

---

Do you know where the majority of serves will fall? Where serves are least likely to fall? What are the implications for the receiving team?

---

the setter faces the on-hand spiker. All five receivers are turned to face the server who must serve from the right rear one-third of the opposite court. Because the server is restricted to serving from the right ten-foot area of his rear court, the receiving alignment is pulled to their left, since it will be virtually impossible for the server to place the ball over the net to the right hand sideline in the front half of the court. The left front, center back and right front players are responsible for receiving any ball which is below waist level in front of, and to the right and left of their starting positions. The left back and right back players are responsible for balls directly in front of them

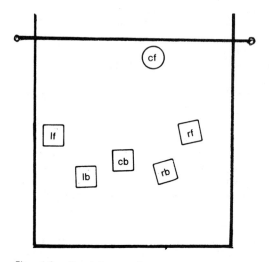

Fig. 4.3   Receiving service

and any ball above waist level for the front line players. The left back takes all balls behind the left front and over the left shoulder of the center back. The right back takes any ball over the center back player's head and right shoulder and beyond the reach of the right front player. In addition, the right and left back players should back up one another.

Each member of the receiving team should take a *stance* which will permit him to move quickly in any direction. It is suggested that all players take a balanced stance with one foot slightly ahead of the other, and with the knees flexed. The hands should be carried about waist high. This is called the "ready position."

Players should be certain to *avoid overlapping positions* when receiving service. It is illegal to overlap with players on either side in the same row or to overlap with the player directly in front or in back of the player in the official line-up positions. For example, the left front and left back may not overlap, the center front and center back may not overlap, and so on.

Defensive Positioning and Movement. When awaiting the ball to be returned by the opponents, the team must be defensively ready. The returned ball will normally move in one of two flight patterns. It will either be spiked forcefully downward or it will be played over in a more lofted arc and with less force. This indicates the necessity for the defensive team to be prepared for either alternative and requires two different choices in defensive positioning to adequately cover the court.

The lofted arc return can be fielded with the forearm pass and converted immediately into the pass-set-spike offense. It becomes evident, however, as opponents develop power and control in the spike that the court coverage to field the spike is increasingly difficult. A well-formed block at the net is required to divert the intentions of the spiker for sound defense.

There are numerous defensive systems used in volleyball. The system suggested in this section is considered to be easily mastered by beginners and one which will most adequately cover the majority of returns that occur in beginning levels of play, namely, the half-speed spike or a "save" play return with a forearm pass. This defense is known as the *center back up* or "dink" defense.

Figure 4.4 shows the *base position* for the center-back-up defense. This position should be taken at the time of one's own team's service or at anytime the ball is returned to the opponents. From this position either the block or the no block defense option can be assumed. Since the *block defense* must develop more quickly the base position anticipates the spike. In the base position all front row players face the net, standing about 45cm from it with hand up at shoulder height. The center back player positions at about midcourt, while the left and right back players position 1-1.5m from the rear lines and 60-90cm from the sidelines.

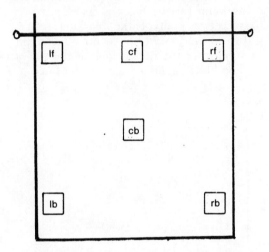

Fig. 4.4   Base position for center back defense

The *no block defense* is used whenever it is anticipated that the opposing spiker cannot execute a hard spike. This defense is used whenever the return is used from mid-court or rear-court, when a set to a spiker is inaccurate so that the spiker is off-balance or poorly positioned, or when the spiker is known to be unable to forcefully spike the ball downward. The player who would normally set the block calls "no block" and the position shown in figure 4.5 is assumed.

The diagram for the *no block defense* shows the position if the ball is returned from the opponents' left front. It should be noted that the center front player, the setter, has stayed near the net out of the way of play so that he may be available to set the ball from the pass. All other players have positioned themselves almost identical to the serve reception "W" formation, with the exception that the formation is turned and adjusted to face the direction of the anticipated return while covering the possible angles of flight for that return. If the return were to be from the center or right side of the opponents' court comparable adjustments to face the direction of the net and coverage of angles would be made.

The effectiveness of a *blocking defense* is dependent upon good blocking mechanics and teamwork. Prior to blocking, the defensive team takes the *base position* shown in figure 4.4. As the ball comes to the opponents' setter, all front row players are within 30-45cm from the net, with vision focused on the ball. As the setter places the ball for the spiker, the blocker directly opposite the spiker assumes the placement of the block directly in front of the ball. Meanwhile the center blocker turns and runs with several long strides toward the side blocker. The two-player block is formed as the center blocker plants the foot nearest the side blocker and pivots toward the net with knees bent and weight low ready to jump for the block. As the center blocker approaches, the side blocker crouches with hands in a ready position to thrust upward. (Figure 4.6) The center blocker makes arm or shoulder contact with the side blocker and the jump for the block is coordinated so that there is no more than 8-10cm between all of the blocking hands. The hand nearest the sideline is turned in toward the court to contain the spike. The blockers' hands may reach over the net, as long as the spiker is allowed to first contact the ball. The blockers should absorb the force of

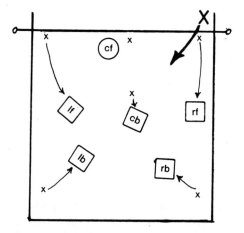

Fig. 4.5 "No block" defense

the recovery to the court by landing on the balls of the feet and flexing the knees and ankles. The hands and arms should be retracted with control to avoid net fouls.

As shown in figure 4.7, as the block is formed, the player at the net who is away from the direction of the set falls away from the net when he sees the set placed, in order to assist in covering the remaining area of the court. As the set is made to the spiker, all nonblocking defensive players are deployed to cover all angles of potential returns past or over the block. The left front and the center back players must be prepared to pick up all soft drop volleys,

Fig. 4.6   The block

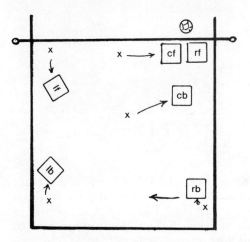

Fig. 4.7   Covering the block (center back up)

or "dinks," over and to the sides of the block as well as partially blocked shots which are deflected into the short court area. In addition, the left front player shares responsibility with the left back player in fielding all spiked balls angled past the block. The left back player positions just to the left of the left shoulder of the center blocker.

If the block is set as described above it should prevent shots down the near sideline. (The various concepts of block placement are presented in the next section.) The right back player, therefore, is responsible to move to any balls which are hit off the blocker's hands or which are hit over the block. In addition, he should be alert to move to cover the appropriate angle should he see that either blocker will be late to the block or will be slow jumping.

Covering the Spiker. The well-executed spike will be "put away" to win a rally at beginning levels of play. As the opponents gain experience in the use of the blocking defense, the offensive team must be alert to react to blocked returns. If the block is successful, the ball may rebound to the spiker's side of the net. Very often the blocked ball will drop over the spiker to the area on the court just behind him. It is necessary for the spiker's teammates to be ready to cover this possibility and to try to reset for another spike and regain the offensive.

The diagram, figure 4.8, indicates the movement of the spiker's teammates when the ball is set to the left front player. All players should be alert,

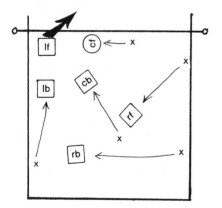

Fig. 4.8   Covering the spiker

in a ready position with the hands carried at waist level. The left back, center back and center front players move in quickly to cover the short block with a semi-circle formation behind the spiker. The right back swings to the left to cover the deep block to the left back area, and the right front moves back to cover the center and right deep court area.

intermediate offensive and defensive concepts

5

Once the basic team strategies are understood and the fundamental skills are mastered, several additional approaches to offense and defense will enhance the excitement of the game. In most instances the tactics offered in this section are built upon an understanding of the basic concepts outlined in the preceding section.

OFFENSE

Four-Two Offensive System. As experience with the game increases it becomes obvious that some players are more effective than others as spikers while some are more valuable as setters. The 4-2 offense is designed to take advantage of the specific strengths of individual players by aligning four spikers and two setters on the court so that there are always one setter and two spikers in the front row. When a spiker rotates to the center front, the setter in the front row *exchanges position* with that spiker by legally *switching* to the center front position.

Which court areas are least well defended in the traditional formation for receiving the serve?

Figure 5.1 shows the *receive of service* positions when the setters are center front and center back, and no switching is required. After one rotation from the original position, the alignment shown in figure 5.2 will be taken to receive the serve. The five player reception formation is identical to that in figure 5.1, except that the center front (spiker) has moved to the position previously taken by the right front. The right front setter moves to the extreme right area near the net, and as soon as the serve is contacted, moves into the center front area to set. The center front spiker functions from the right front position. All players involved in switching must hold position until the serve is contacted so that overlapping does not occur. This includes not

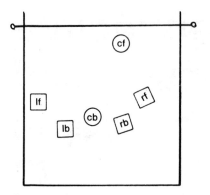

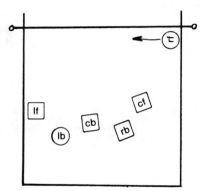

Fig. 5.1   Receiving service, 4-2 offense

Fig. 5.2   Receiving service, 4-2 offense with setter's switch

only the center front and right front players, but also the position of the center back player in relation to the center front player. Since the center front player has pulled back to assist in receiving serve, he must be certain to be positioned nearer the net than the center back player.

When the team rotates another position, it will be noted from figure 5.2 the right front setter will move to the back row and the left back setter will move to the front row in the left front position. When the setter is in the left front for reception of service, he positions near the net and as near the sideline as possible, while the center front player pulls back to cover the left front receiving position. After the ball is contacted on the service the setter moves to the center front area and the center front player functions as the left front spiker. It must be remembered that if a switch has occurred, all players must return to original positions prior to each service.

The *switch for the serving team* is always much easier than for the receiving team since the ball must be returned before the ball is to be played. Figure 5.3 illustrates the left front setter and center front spiker switch. The two players position near one another and after the ball is contacted on the service each player moves to the base position for defense at the net.

Service Tactics. The most important factor in maintaining an offensive advantage is a well-placed service. If the serve falls into the uncovered spaces of the court the result is an immediate score. If the serve results in passing errors, the receiving team will be less able to develop a potent offense.

Several court areas are vulnerable in the traditional serve reception formation. The deep side lines areas are very vulnerable. If the serve is executed with either floating or spinning action, the resultant pass is often played toward the out-of-bounds area where there is no one readily available to play the next hit.

The deep center back court area is also vulnerable in that it causes the left and right back players to coordinate the coverage. If either player hesitates, the serve may fall in for a point, or the pass may be poorly placed. Short serves which clear the net within .6-1m from net height are placed

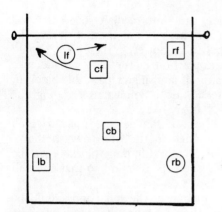

Fig. 5.3   4-2 offense—switch for
the serving team

to the areas between the right front and center back, or between the center back and the left front often create handling errors for the receiving team. The short serve has a very small margin of error, but the server who has mastered control of it through practice has a decided advantage.

Another aspect of vulnerability can be discovered in an analysis of the passing abilities of the receiving team players. Serves placed to the weaker passers can result in costly passing errors.

Finally, consideration of the position of the receiving team's strongest spikers is important. A serve placed to the side of the court away from the strongest spiker in the front row will cause the pass to be taken by the setter so that a less reliable back set must be utilized to get the set to that strong spiker.

Setting Tactics. Setting is the key to sound offensive volleyball. The setter who keeps track of all the game circumstances may often create an advantage for the offense by advantageously placing the ball for the spiker.

The setter should have a good knowledge of the spikers on his own team with regard to abilities as well as desires in types of sets, and should attempt to adjust sets accordingly.

It is also imperative that the setter know the opposing team. The attempt should be made to set away from the opponents' strongest blockers, while setting to the opponents' blocking weaknesses.

The competent setter will work to develop basic technique in setting which will not tip off the direction or type of set to the opposing team. This is vital in fooling the block. The effective setter will also seek to move the sets to both sides of the court, using maximum court width so that the blockers will be forced to move rapidly to cover the play.

When the setter is off-balance due to a bad pass the attempt should be made to set to the easiest position possible, which is usually a front set. If the spiker has been placed off-balance or has been slow in the spike approach due to fatigue, the setter should set the ball slightly higher than usual to assist the spiker in timing the approach.

Spike Variations. At the beginning and early intermediate stages of learning to spike the player will see nothing but the ball and the net during the approach and jump to spike. With experience, however, the spiker should begin utilizing peripheral vision to see the position of the blockers and take advantage by placing the spike at the appropriate angles past the block or through the holes in the block. This technique is known as "reading the block."

In addition, the thinking spiker will check the defense prior to each service to see how the blockers have positioned in the front row so that a slow moving blocker, a short blocker or a poor jumping blocker can be spotted. The backcourt defense should also be kept in mind so that the ball can be placed to an open space.

The effective spiker will have full command of the spike and should be able to choose the angle of the spike at the latest possible moment. The spiker should always be prepared to dink the ball to an open space or hit a half-speed spike to catch the defense off balance. These tactics are especially deceiving when used by a strong spiker, because the defense cannot adequately cover all the alternatives of his potential actions.

Finally, the spiker who is developing in ability should work to use the blockers' hands to win points. A spike placed to hit off the outside hand of the side line blocker will usually rebound out of bounds out of reach of the defense.

Line-up Considerations. The line-up is established with thought given to both offensive and defensive abilities of players. The type of offense used will also dictate certain factors. With the 4-2 offense the following factors are usually considered.

With two spikers and one setter in the front row at all times, usually the strongest spiker starts in the left front, with the second strongest spiker starting in the right back position. This assures the team of having one strong spiker in the front row at all times. The other two spikers are placed in relation to their respective serving and defensive abilities.

The first two or three servers in the line-up should possess strong serves. The strongest blockers should start left back, left front and center front, while the players starting right front, right back and center back should be strong in backcourt defense since these are the positions in the line-up which will usually be confronted with the opponents' strongest attack.

In the 4-2 offense the setters can be started either in the center positions or at either of the side positions. If the spiker is especially effective on the on-hand side that spiker should lead the adjacent setter in the line-up since this will switch that spiker to the on-hand side when the spiker is center front.

DEFENSE

Blocking Tactics. The placement of the block is critical to a soundly functioning defense. There are two basic placements. In the first, the block is set to *give the line* to the spiker. This means that the block will be established to take away the majority of the wider cross court angle space, and invite the spiker to hit to the much narrower area between the block and the sideline. This can be seen in figure 5.4. This tactic is very effective against the beginning spiker since he often cannot adequately place the hit down the sideline at will, and will almost invariably spike cross court into the block.

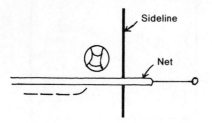

Fig. 5.4   Giving the line

The second block placement is that of *taking the line*. This can be seen in figure 5.5. This block is designed to force all spikes into the cross court angle. Usually this block placement is accompanied by strong backcourt coverage into the cross court area past the block to field the spikes which are not contained by the block.

The *attack block* is an offensive use of the block. It requires that the blockers be able to jump well and have good body control. As the block is formed the blockers reach the hands and forearms well over the net in an umbrella-like position over the spike, meeting the ball with the firm forward thrust before retracting the hands and returning to the court. The result is a spiked ball which is blocked forcefully down to the court with little chance of the spiker's teammates retrieving it.

Center-back-deep Defense. In the first section of the chapter a team defense is presented which is strong in coverage of the spike, soft hits and dinks, but which is vulnerable in the deep center back area of the court. An alternate defense is the center-back-deep defense which is strong in blocking the spike and in deep back court coverage, but somewhat vulnerable to the dink. The choice in defenses depends on the strengths of the opponents.

The base position for this defense is shown in figure 5.6. It will be noted that all base positions are identical to those in figure 5.6 except for the center back player who starts in the back line in the middle of the court.

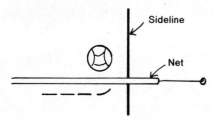

Fig. 5.5   Taking the line

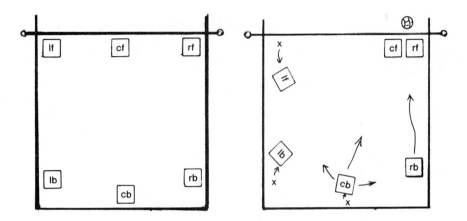

Fig. 5.6 Base position for center-back-deep defense

Fig. 5.7 Covering the block (center-back-deep)

Figure 5.7 illustrates the blocking of a spike from the opposing left front. As the block is set the left front pulls away from the net and is alert to field the acutely angled shot past the block or a soft hit short to the center of the court. The left back positions just outside the left shoulder of the center blocker to field the hard hit spikes past the block. The center back player takes a position on a line from the ball to the spot between the two blockers. He is responsible for all balls rebounding off the block deep to the back court or any ball, hit over or through the block. The right back player covers the line. If the block "gives the line" this player must hold position until it can be seen whether or not the spiker will hit to the line. If the block "takes the line" this player can charge forward to cover behind the block for dinks and soft deflections off the block.

Defensive Switching. It is possible to make interchanges of position on the court after the service to better deploy defensive players to take advantage of specific defensive abilities. These switches are quite simple when executed by the serving team. When executed by the receiving team these switches are usually done as the players move from the cover of their own spiker into their base positions for defense. Only the most necessary switches should be attempted after receiving service and spiking, since confusion can easily occur and disrupt the offense.

advanced skills

6

Volleyball has been identified as the most popular participant sport in America. It should be recognized, however, that this statement includes all levels of play and varieties of conditions. Enjoyment is possible with rather limited skills but as the players improve their skills the satisfaction derived from the game increases many-fold. As the skill level increases, attention to the "fine points" of the game becomes a necessity. The following material is presented with the thought that while beginners may have some difficulty in executing advanced movement skills effectively, it is necessary to understand them in order to make them ultimately a part of your game.

COURT SENSE

Probably the most critical skill for you to learn is "court sense." Court sense is the ability to be in the right place at the right time by reacting to your opponent's game so that you are always in good position for either offensive or defensive play. Better players continually adjust their positions during play even when they do not appear to be directly involved in the action. They are always ready for the unexpected. They are actually calculating the probability that the opponent will follow a predictable course of action. As more information develops the play predicts the options for the spiker and the defensive player moves to a position which will optimize the chances for fielding the ball. A spiker, on the other hand, develops the ability to "read the block." This advanced skill will determine whether the spiker should hit crosscourt, down the line, over the block or even use a "dink" that will drop the ball just behind the blockers. The ability to make this last second decision marks the advanced player.

The development of court sense is speeded up if you get into the habit of determining how you can position yourself on each play in order to be most effective. Think about the elements of the game. Ask yourself, "Was I in the best possible position during the rally?" Remember that these automatic adjustments require constant attention to the details of the action of play.

SETTING VARIATIONS

The *back set* is one of the skills more easily executed after the fundamental set has been developed. The purpose of the back set is deception. The setter faces one direction and then proceeds to set the ball back overhead to a spiker who is approaching to hit the ball. The starting position is identical to the front set with a forward-back stride and knees flexed. However, at the last moment the setter arches the back slightly, drawing the body forward. This causes the ball to be contacted just over the crown of the head. The hands and arms are extended upward to meet the ball with the follow-through overhead and the weight shifted to the rear foot.

The *shoot set* is also a deceptive technique requiring much practice coordination between the setter and the spiker. The set is pushed forward in an arc almost parallel to the top of the net. The setter's execution is not difficult. It simply involves allowing the ball to drop to a position in front of the forehead as the vision is focussed forward rather than upward. The ball is aimed so that it reaches the spiker at about 30-40cm above net height. This is classified as an advanced technique because of the demand for accuracy and the difficulty that exists for a spiker to learn to hit this set with consistency.

The *short set* is also used to deceive the blockers. It can be used at any position at the net, but is most commonly used as a set to the center spiker in the multiple offense. The pass to the setter must be near perfect. The setter simply extends elbows and wrist with very little leg extension. The ball is softly lifted directly upward to a height of approximately 40-45cm above the net height. As in the shoot set, the difficulty lies in consistency and timing with the spiker.

Standing at left front court about 1m from the net, toss the ball 1-2m above net height and about 4-5m from the net. Can you jump and spike the ball to the diagonally opposite backcourt? up the sideline on the same side of the court? Can you do these from a set up from a teammate?

SPIKING VARIATIONS

Spiking the ball is, for most beginners, a very difficult skill to master because it depends upon several critical factors. First a good set is necessary. Only very advanced players learn to hit the "'bad" ball while almost anyone can learn to hit a good set. The would-be spiker must learn to move away from the net so that he can hit the ball out in front of his body. Most beginners get caught at the net with the set coming down over their head. When this happens the tendency is to reach over the head and try to hit the ball. Rarely is the ball driven down; usually it is bumped high and slowly goes to the opponent where it is easily fielded. You simply cannot develop a powerful hit if you extend your arm over your head to hit the ball. You must cock the arm and lead out with the elbow just as you do when you throw a ball hard.

The volleyball must be contacted well out in front of the shoulder so that the heel of the hand strikes above and behind the center of gravity of the ball.

The *dink* is also a deceptive offensive tactic. The spiker makes a normal approach and jump to spike. However, at the last moment the elbow of the hitting arm is extended with the wrist firm and fingers extended. The ball is softly contacted with the finger tips, placing it over or to sides of the block. The key to success in executing this tactic is keeping the elbow extended and the wrist firm to avoid "throwing" the ball.

Fig. 6.1 Dink

Spiking the shoot set requires an adaptation of the normal spiking approach. It is hit from the on-hand position because the set moves laterally in front of the spiker it would be difficult to time the contact of the ball at the exact moment it was in front of the hitting shoulder. The adjustment is made by the spiker moving forward and outside the court to a shallow distance from the net. The approach is then made parallel to the net, moving toward the oncoming ball. The spike is executed by swinging the arm across the body, directing the ball into the opponents' court.

Spiking the short set may be the most difficult technique to master in the game. It requires that the spiker start slightly nearer the net than in the regular spike. The approach is begun while the pass is approaching the setter.

Fig. 6.2 Hitting the short set

The spiker approaches toward a position directly in front of the setter, jumping into the air as the setter pushes the set upward. The spiker's arm swings and intercepts the flight of the set. Timing of both players' movements is critical and requires hours of practice.

Many of the better defensive players have acquired skills at recovering their position after having committed themselves to an extreme effort to field the ball that has resulted in a loss of balance. One of these maneuvers is *the roll*. Although there are a number of variations to this technique, the basic format involves continuing the reach for the ball even though falling down becomes necessary. The fall then must be converted into a sequence which results in a dissipation of the shock as a consequence of rolling to spread the impact out over a longer time base. No one part of the body takes the blow. The momentum of the fall is then used to provide the energy for a recovery to the feet. Thus, learning to fall without sustaining injury becomes an advanced skill in volleyball.

The *dive* is an alternative technique used to move a ball that is well beyond the reach of the player. The player runs as far as possible, moving quickly to a position with the head and shoulders well ahead of the feet. The diving movement is then made parallel to the surface of the court, with one or both arms extending fully to a position under the ball. The feet kick up-

Fig. 6.3   The roll

ward from the floor as the back is arched. The arms then snap down quickly
to catch the body weight, lowering the chest to the floor as the elbows bend.
The arms then thrust backward causing the torso to slide on the court to
absorb the remainder of the force of the body weight. It is important to observe safety precautions in this technique. The dive should be learned in a
progression, first from a hands and knees position, then from a squatting
position before moving to the full dive. The head should be tilted backward
throughout the action to avoid hitting the chin on the court surface upon
impact. Also, work should be done to develop arm and shoulder strength prior
to attempting the dive.

Fig. 6.4 The dive

advanced offensive and defensive concepts

7

Numerous teams competing at the advanced level of play do so using the basic and intermediate tactics described in the preceding sections. The difference between intermediate and advanced play often is the consistently excellent performance of the fundamental skills and tactics by the advanced level player. In addition to excellence in performance, some advanced teams use more intricate offenses than those outlined above. These offenses demand some countering defensive considerations.

How are the setting and spiking duties divided among the team players in the 6-2 multiple offense? Where do the setter spikers start? When do they act as spikers?

Multiple Offense. The multiple offense utilizes all three front row players as spikers. The setter is a back row player who moves into the right front area, about 3m in from the right sideline, and chooses to front set to either of two on-hand spikers (left front or center front), or back set to the off-hand spiker (right front). The fact that the offense now has three potential spikers, coupled with the deceptive setting variations and decoying movements by the spikers, creates many problems for the defensive team.

There are three different team approaches to the multiple offense—the 5-1, 6-0 and 6-2 offenses. The *5-1 offense* is one in which the team has five spikers and one setter. The setter starts in the right back position as shown in figure 7.1. As the ball is contacted by the server the setter runs into the right front passing area. Figure 7.2 illustrates the movement when the setter has rotated to the center back. When the setter becomes the left back, the movement to the right side passing area is difficult, so an alternate choice would be to set from the left front area with the setter facing two off-hand spikers as shown in figure 7.3. As the setter rotates to the front row the offense becomes identical to a 4-2 offense with the setter switching into the center front. This 4-2 type offense continues until the setter again rotates into the right back position.

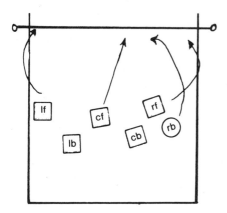

Fig. 7.1   Receiving service, 5-1 offense, setter from right back

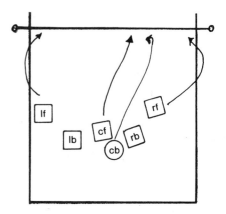

Fig. 7.2   Receiving service, 5-1 offense, setter from center back

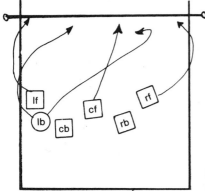

Fig. 7.3   Receiving service, 5-1 offense, setter from left back

The *6-0 offense* is based on the multiple attack of three spikers in the front row, but demands that each spiker also be a capable setter. Each spiker, upon reaching the right back position, runs into the front row as a setter as shown in figure 7.1.

In the *6-2 offense* the team is composed of four spikers and two setter-spikers. The setter-spikers start opposite one another, and when in the back row function as a setter, but upon reaching the front row function as a spiker.

Setting Variations for Multiple Offense. The regular set described in preceding sections is used in the multiple offense, but is accompanied by other set variations which are designed to deceive the blockers.

When the setter receives a good pass he has the option of setting a short front set to the center front player or a short back set to the right front player. The short set can vary from an extremely low set placed with the bottom of the ball only 20-25cm from the top of the net, to a slightly higher set with the bottom of the ball 40-50cm above the top of the net. Both sets require that the spiker approach and jump into the air with the arm cocked before being able to see where the set is placed. The setter virtually places the set to the spiker's hitting hand. Since the spiker commits himself to approach and jump before the set, should the setter choose not to set to that spiker and set to one of the other spikers, the faked approach and jump become a very distracting and decoying factor to the defense.

The *shoot set* is another variation in which the set travels in a low arc just above and almost parallel to the net tape. The spiker intercepts the ball in its flight and drives it into the opponents' court.

Spiking both the short set and the shoot set requires hours of practice to perfect the timing and execution. The setter is usually unable to execute these sets unless he receives almost perfect passing, therefore, these tactics are not recommended for use until the team members have mastered the basic techniques.

Signals are used between the spiker and the setter to indicate when these variations are to be used. The signal can be given visually prior to a pass to the setter, or verbally during the pass to the setter.

Defense Against the Multiple Offense. The basic team defenses described in earlier sections are used at advanced levels also. To counter-act the multiple offense, however, the blockers are often required to block one-on-one if the offense is extremely deceptive. If the direction of the set can be read, a two player block can be formed. To counter-act the center spike a one or two player block can be formed, depending on the spiking tendencies of the hitter, while the remaining defensive players attempt to cover the backcourt area at angles past the block.

Since the multiple offense setting variations require excellent passing, one of the best defenses against them is a strong offense and serve. These will keep the opponents off-balance while passing and therefore less able to generate a strong offense.

Transition from Offense to Defense. The setter who has run into the front row from the back row may not participate in the block. After the offense has returned the ball to the opponents the setter returns to the back row. In order that this transition be made smoothly, the setter always moves to a prearranged position depending on the defense employed by his team. If the center-back-deep defense is used the setter switches into the right back position. If the center-back-up defense is used the setter becomes the player under the block, or the center back. From these positions the movement back and forth from offense to defense is simplified.

coeducational
play

8

Coeducational play presents slightly different problems than those encountered in men's or women's volleyball. Usually the men attempt to absorb the power aspects of the game. Therefore the men form the basic receiving formation on the service and form a two player block on defense with the third man in position to field the hard hit ball past the block. The women function as setters, and on defense cover the block and the court angles to field the softer placement shots and balls which are deflected by the block. Since the net is 25m high the women are rarely used as spikers.

Receiving Service and Offense. The diagrams in figure 8.1 and 8.2 show the serve reception formations for the two situations in co-ed play. With two men in the front row the pass is made to the woman in the center front who is the setter, while the spikers hit from the left and right front areas. With one man in the front row the spiker may choose to hit from the center or may swing to the right or left front areas, depending on the direction of the pass. Either front row woman is the setter.

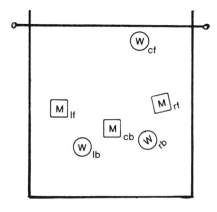

Fig. 8.1 COED—receiving service with two men in front row

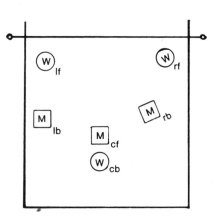

Fig. 8.2 COED—receiving service with one man in front row

Defense Against the Spike. Defense for strong spiking in mixed volleyball presents some interesting problems. Not only do the men absorb the power aspects of the game, but they must often block after moving great distances to get in position to do so. In addition, the strategy demands a great deal of switching of the men and women. The reader is encouraged to carefully study the diagrams so that the switches can be noted. Care must also be taken to avoid overlapping.

The defense presented here is one of several which could be employed. This defense is built on the concept that a two man block is always used. The block is always placed so that it *takes the line* (figure 5.5) *on the opponent's on-hand side* (block at own right front), and that the block always *gives the line* (Figure 5.4) *on the opponent's off-hand side* (block at own left front). With this positioning the third man (not blocking) is always positioned in the left back area. From there he fields the hard hits on the crosscourt angles from the opponent's on-hand, and the hard hits down the line on the opponent's off-hand.

The base position for this defense is shown in figure 8.3. The actual positions of player for the defense depends upon the rotation. With two men in the front row, figure 8.4 shows the position at service with the arrows indi-

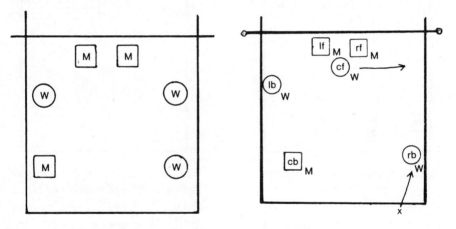

Fig. 8.3   COED—base position for drill

Fig. 8.4   COED—switch for defense with two men in front row

cating the movement to the base positions. Figures 8.5 and 8.6 indicate the block and coverage for the spike at the opponent's on-hand and off-hand sides, respectively.

With the rotation placing one man in the front row, the same base position is taken on defense, but players come from different positions than shown here. Figure 8.7 shows the position at the time for service with arrows indicating the movement to the base positions. Figures 8.8 and 8.9 show the block and coverage of the back court for the opponent's on-hand and off-hand spikes, respectively.

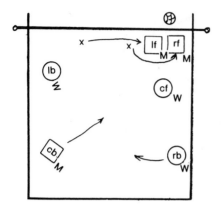

Fig. 8.5   COED—block for opponents'
on-hand spike with two men in front row

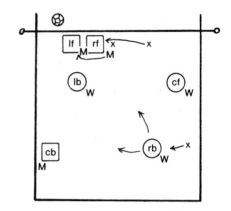

Fig. 8.6   COED—block for opponents'
off-hand spike with one man in front row

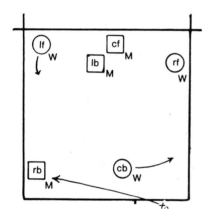

Fig. 8.7   COED—switch for defense
with one man in front row

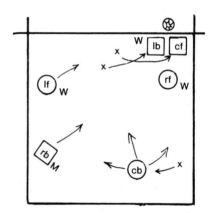

Fig. 8.8   COED—block for opponents'
on-hand spike with one man in front
row

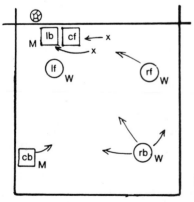

Fig. 8.9   COED—block for opponents' off-hand
spike with one man in front row

THE SPIRIT OF TEAM PLAY

If a team is to be successful it is necessary for all members to play the game to the limits of their abilities. The thrill of a good performance can be experienced again and again by the player who is mentally alert, and who will make every possible effort to carry out his assignments. An even greater thrill is in store for the player who will seek, through his own play, to enhance the performance of his teammate. Complete confidence in, and respect for one's teammate is the basis of real team play.

improving individual performance

9

It is important to recognize that competitive volleyball requires an understanding of the many factors which can affect performance during play. As skill improves, these factors tend to become more important. Therefore, to play effectively one must prepare effectively for the specific requirements of the sport. Let us look at a few of these factors.

Since volleyball requires rapid movement and a great deal of swinging and stretching it is necessary to wear clothing which does not restrict movement through the full range of movement. Restrictive clothing can result in handicapped speed, timing and range of motion. Adequate footwear should be lightweight, comfortable and above all should fit so that rapid starts and stops do not produce foot discomfort or blisters.

The use of knee pads, elbow pads and garments which bind across joints should also be evaluated to maximize freedom of movement.

The development of adequate levels of strength and endurance to meet the demands of the game must be based upon an analysis of game components. In brief, one must develop strength and endurance in the functional muscle groups within the range of motion in which they are actually used and under nearly identical metabolic conditions. The high degree of specificity in training requirements is now becoming fully appreciated and older concepts of generalized strength and endurance training have been replaced with the concept of training for the identical elements of performance which will be found in competitive play.

In what three ways can muscle groups be overloaded? What advantage is there in the use of isokinetic devices in weight training?

The training concept is fairly straightforward. In order to improve strength and endurance levels for volleyball one must overload the functional muscle groups in a manner identical to their *intended* use. If an individual can overload the muscles by increasing resistance and speed of movement during an imitation of a skill, the strength and endurance components required for that act will benefit directly to the performance.

Overloading can be the result of increasing resistance or intensity, rate of work or duration of work. The selection of the overloading should be based upon the elements of the skill and should be progressive i.e. do more work today than you did yesterday. Steady improvement, not necessarily dramatic, should be expected over several weeks or even months. Gains are generally more rapid when the trainee is at a lower level of capability. As one's training level improves, the rate of change will tend to level off.

The following recommendations for a resistance training are based upon an analysis of the general movements used in the game situation. The selection of the type of resistance will usually be dependent upon the availability of apparatus, weights and numbers of persons working out.

An analysis of the jumping requirements of the game can provide an example for this specificity concept. There are several types of jumps used in volleyball for various purposes. The jumping techniques for blocking and spiking differ significantly from the biomechanical point of view and neither variation has much in common with a jump from a full squat position. Therefore, the use of heavy weights in training from a full squat while effectively increasing strength in the knee and hip extensors, would be concentrating the development at a point in the range of motion at less than 90° of flexion of the knee. The volleyball player would rarely use this position for initiating a jump. At the same time, a less intense resistance would be present at approximately 120° of knee and hip extension, where most volleyball jumps would begin.

Isometric strength training techniques could be used to develop strength at particular points in the range of motion. For example, the athlete can squat in a position simulating preparation for a jump and a padded bar could be fixed at an appropriate height to permit the jumper to exert a near maximal force in the intended direction of the jump. Holding this near maximal contraction for 10-15 seconds and repeating the effort several times daily should result in increased strength for the jump.

It is important to provide the overload in a manner consistent with the development of the summation of forces involved in the action being developed. The use of constant friction devices such as exergenie or iso-kinetic devices which allow the resistance to be selectively placed in the range of motion offer a significant advantage over traditional weight training routines.

The acquisition of skill can be enhanced through repetitive practice which is specific to game conditions. Environmental conditions such as conditions of the floor, lighting, obstructions, temperature, noise levels can affect performance and should be considered by those who wish to maximize performance. Some of this consideration would appear to be psychologic which leads to a further observation. It is necessary to overlearn critical skills to a point where they are nearly automatic. Once the skill has been overlearned it is important to provide reinforcement periodically in order to insure that a high level of effectiveness is maintained. There are several techniques which can be used to speed up progress toward the goal of overlearned skills.

Efficient and effective movement on the court becomes easier when appropriate methods for the action are used. As an example, the individual who is standing upright with feet fairly close together, arms extended will not be able to move as efficiently as the individual who widens the base of support, flexes the knees slightly and carries the hands below the shoulders. In the latter position the weight can be shifted quickly to the driving leg and a powerful extension combined with a general shifting of the center of mass in the desired direction makes a significant difference in the move. Thus the volleyball player who must take steps to get to the ball is well advised to run first, then reach.

As playing techniques are learned it is very important to learn proper mechanics for the skills. Frequently a player will learn an inefficient technique and become very effective in spite of the poor technique. The question arises, how much more effective would the performer become using better technique and it is worth the effort of retraining? The question is often difficult to answer.

The use of resistance in the development of strength for a skilled activity should be preceded by a careful consideration of the desired training and conditioning goals. The many studies on resistance training have generally pointed out that weight training can be effective in developing specific strength in functional muscle groups used in specific sports. It appears that lower repetition-higher intensity training has a greater strength benefit while higher repetition-lower intersity training has a greater endurance benefit. In both cases there is a training effect which indicates that strength and endurance training are not mutually exclusive. The key then appears to be "emphasis." The emphasis needed in the various aspects of volleyball skill appears to be primarily in "explosive" moves such as quick starts, jumps and changes of direction. The strength demands then are high with an emphasis on speed.

Monroe, in an unpublished master's thesis study was able to demonstrate a statistically significant increase in the speed of a spike after a six week training program involving resistance.

The resistance should be applied early in the movement range of motion in order to affect the summation of forces in trunk rotation, shoulder rotation and elbow extension. An effective device for this type of training is the friction pulley which permits a constant resistance through a full range of motion. A simple device for such resistance consists of a smooth section of pipe mounted about 30cm above head height. A 1/4" - 5/16" diameter nylon rope is fitted with a handle and wound around the pipe, each loop around the pipe provides additional resistance. A small weight is then hung on the end of the rope in contact with the pipe. Additional resistance can be obtained by increasing the counter weight.

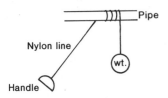

Fig. 9.1   A friction pulley

It is particularly important to duplicate the movement as nearly identical to the game skill as possible. Attention to hip, trunk, shoulder, elbow and wrist is critical to obtaining an effective duplication of the desired movement.

The same type of resistive device can be used to strengthen other important moves used in the game.

There are a number of small, portable friction devices which are available commercially which can be fastened to such things as doors, posts, stairs, etc., and which will allow great flexibility in permitting the duplication of various movements against increasing amounts of resistance.

It is also recommended that resistance training be scheduled along with the conduct of regular performance of the skills. This will insure that timing and coordination of the skill will progress along with the strength increases.

A technique for improving individual play that has been used quite effectively involves learning to play with progressively fewer players on a side.

The teams play with the customary six on a side until the rules and most fundamentals of the game are understood. Then the teams are reduced to five on a side for two or three periods of practice, then four, three and finally two. If this progression is timed appropriately, the players become accustomed to moving quickly to the ball and making their passes and sets more effective. After moving through the progression (four to six weeks), the players are reorganized to six on a side. The resultant play is usually dramatically improved since players have learned about the importance of readiness to move and court position. This form of practice also incorporates the improvement of conditioning in a game situation.

Effective serve placement can be developed if the server imagines a six-part division of the court and practices dropping his serve in each one of the six divisions. The skill developed in this kind of practice will enable the server to follow weaker fielders from position to position and force them to move to their weak side to field the ball. Accuracy in serving can also be improved if the server develops a consistent pattern for handling the ball during the preparation for service. This includes details such as the placement of the valve, since the valve causes a slight imbalance which can affect the flight of the ball.

A self-improvement technique which has been helpful in bettering the skills of many new players is called mental practice. This form of practice requires that the individual focus his concentration on patterns of movement he has learned; he introspectively rehearses the skill to be improved. For example, in improving the spike one could introspectively rehearse timing the moving ball with the jump to proper height and the body movements involved in hitting and following through. It has been suggested in various experimental studies that such introspective rehearsal can result in marked improvements in skill. It is a practice widely used by high level performers and can be applied when the individual is away from the game. The focus of concentration can also be helpful in developing the court sense, or the ability to know where and when to move, since you can analyze imagined game situations involving a variety of problems.

The development of specific skills and fundamental maneuvers can best be accomplished by practicing them purposefully in drills which are game-like.

Following are examples of how fundamentals can be incorporated into patterns which will be similar to game situations. The symbol key is as follows:

————————➤ Passed ball

-O—O➤ Player moves

– – – –➤ Set ball

Ⓥ Spike or serve

Fig. 9.2   The symbol key

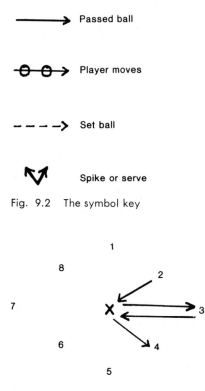

Fig. 9.3   The passing drill

1. The formation in figure 9.3 is used to practice passing and setting to various distances and locations. Center player passes to each player in the formation. At the conclusion of a full circuit center then moves to #2 while #1 moves to the center; all other players move one position clockwise.

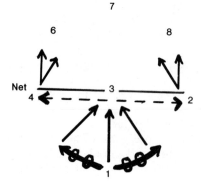

Fig. 9.4   The multiple skill drill

2. The formation in figure 9.4 can be used to practice pass, set, spike and blocking or digging. The pass from #1 is received by #3 who sets to either #2 or #4 for a spike. The defense can field the ball or attempt a two- or three-man block. All players rotate after two or three turns in the same position. Note: bad passes to the setter and bad sets to the spiker should be played as if a point were at stake.

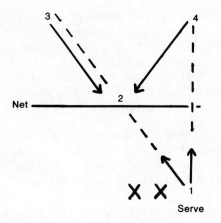

Fig. 9.5   Game situation drill

3. The formation in figure 9.5 uses service, service receiving and passing.

   It is important to remember that the drills should involve the application of skill in ways very similar or identical to the game situation and that the same effort should be put into practice as into a game.

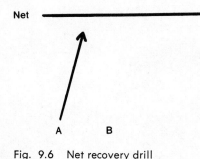

Fig. 9.6   Net recovery drill

4. A simple drill for developing ability to recover balls from the net is shown in figure 9.6.

   Player A passes the ball into the net at various heights and distances from player B who must then move into position to field it and bump it into the air, preferably as a set since the ball in the net usually occurs on a bad pass and only one hit will remain after the recovery.

The development of strength and endurance for improved play can be developed if attention is paid to a few basic concepts. First, the analysis of the players movements must be made in order to establish which major functional muscle groups are being used. These functional muscle groups should then be worked to maximal levels and subsequently *overloaded.* That is, they must be progressively worked harder and harder while going through the identical ranges of motion required during play. This overloading can be accomplished by increasing the intensity of the exercise through the use of additional resistance. Several kinds of apparatus using weights, springs, pulleys, etc., can be used.

The strength in jumping, for example, can be developed by jumping into the air from a ¾ squat position, while carrying weight on the shoulders or around the waist. The jumper could overload by increasing the weight he carries, increasing the number of times he jumps or decreasing the time it would take to jump a given number of times. It is important to jump in the same manner that would be used in the game. During this type of training it is also important to practice the movement under normal conditions.

The arm action in spiking can be duplicated on wall pulley apparatus or on friction pulleys such as the Exergenie. The movement through the range of motion against a resistance will result in increased strength and endurance if the conditioning is carried out in a conscientious manner.

Increasing the resistance progressively over a period of several weeks is important. If the players work to the limits of their strength and continually strive to work just a little harder each time the training effect can be dramatic and play can improve as a result.

Overloading can also be applied by increasing the duration of the training program or by increasing the rate at which the players are required to work. If the players keep track of their progress they will know that they are getting stronger, have more endurance, and are quicker and more effective in their play.

Remember that the player must condition himself for the *specific* muscular and skill requirements of volleyball. Practice does not necessarily make perfect performance. *Only perfect practice leads to perfect performance.*

organization of the sport

10

Volleyball in the United States is played at every conceivable level of skill. The international competition is well regulated by the United States Volleyball Association, which is affiliated with all the organizations within which volleyball is played. The country is divided into fifteen regions which have an internal administration for tournaments.

Within the regions the men and women play in graded competition with AA being the highest. Tournaments are regularly scheduled and teams are drawn from such areas as the Armed Forces, YMCA, athletic clubs, schools, colleges, playgrounds and private enterprises.

Team matches are also scheduled and usually go to the best three of five games. These matches generally do not have any bearing on team standings unless they are scheduled in league play.

Outside the framework of formal competition, one can participate in volleyball at athletic clubs, playgrounds and in schools. It is common practice for one or two nights to be devoted to volleyball in most public or semipublic facilities. Usually the level of play and whether the play is for men's, women's, or mixed groups are designated. Many public facilities schedule adult volleyball which excludes individuals below eighteen for a particular time period.

During the summer months parks and beaches become ideal places to engage in the sport and the level of play improves as the season progresses. The spectator who would like to watch competitive volleyball can write to the United States Volleyball Regional Representative in your area. Addresses and other pertinent information are contained in the Official Guide. This annual rule book and reference guide is published by the USVBA and can be obtained by sending $2.50 plus postage to:

U.S.V.B.A. PRINTER
Box 109
Berne, Indiana 46711

A variety of teaching and training aids are available to improve performance. These devices are discussed in various contributions to an expanding literature. A selected bibliography is included in order to assist the enthusiast. A more complete bibliography can be obtained through the USVB National Headquarters, 557 Fourth St., San Francisco, ca. 94107.

selected
bibliography

1. 1977 Annual Official Volleyball Rules and Reference Guide of the United States Volleyball Association. Available from U.S.V.B.A. Printer, Box 109, Berne, Indiana.
2. KELLER, VAL. *Point, Game and Match.* Creative Sports Books, Hollywood, Ca. 1968.
3. KELLER, VAL. *Point, Game and Match — Coaching Supplement.* Creative Sports Books, P.O. Box 2244, Hollywood, ca. 90028, 1971.
4. LENAIR, JULIEN. "The World's Championship," Bulletin Oficiel (Mar. 1957), pg. 12.
5. PLOTNICKI, BEN A. "Brief History of Volleyball," University of Tennessee, 70th U.S.V.B.A. Guide, 1965 (U.S.V.B.A., Berne, Indiana), pg. 27-28.
6. SANDEFUR, RANDY. *Volleyball.* Pacific Palisades, California: Goodyear Publishing Company, 1970.
7. SCATES, ALLEN E., and WARD, JANE. *Volleyball.* Boston: Allyn and Bacon, Inc., 1969.
8. SCHAAFSMA, FRANCES and HECK, ANN. *Volleyball for Coaches and Teachers.* Dubuque, Iowa: Wm. C. Brown Company, 1971.
9. 1978 Annual Official Volleyball Rules and Reference Guide of the United States Volleyball Association. Available: U.S.V.B.A. Printer, Box 109, Berne, Indiana.
10. WELCH, J. EDMUND, (ed.). "How to Play and Teach Volleyball" (N.Y. Association Press, 1960), pg. 55, 61.
11. DUNPHY, MARV., *Volleyball,* Grosset and Dunlap, Inc., 1977.
12. MONROE, MARY DIANE, "the effect of Overload Training on Accuracy and speed of the Volleyball Spike." M.S. thesis, U.C.L.A. Department of Physical Education. 1971.

questions
and answers

MULTIPLE CHOICE

1. An official size court is:
   a. 15m × 7m b. 18m × 9m c. 16m × 10m (p. 1)

2. The first serve is determined by:
   a. toss of coin b. visiting team c. referees choice (p. 12)

3. A game is completed when one team scores:
   a. 15 points
   b. 7 points more than the opponent
   c. 15 points to opponents' 13 points or fewer (p. 12)

4. Net height for men's play is:
   a. 2.13m b. 2.33m c. 2.43m (p. 10)

5. Net height for women's play is:
   a. 2.13m b. 2.24m c. 2.31m (p. 10)

6. The overhand serve, if delivered correctly, will:
   a. be a hard drive down the line c. land on the back court line
   b. float or wobble over the net (p. 18)

7. The most difficult serve to return is a well hit:
   a. overhand b. underhand c. roundhouse (p. 19)

8. Generally, the most consistent serve, but easiest to return is the:
   a. overhand b. underhand c. roundhouse (p. 20)

9. The best spot to contact the ball in an overhand serve is:
   a. behind and slightly below the center of mass
   b. behind and directly even with the center of the mass
   c. slightly to the right side below the center of mass (p. 20)

10. In an underhand serve the ball:
    a. rests on the left hand if hit by the right hand
    b. is hit by the heel or flat of the fist of the hand it rests on
    c. is tossed into the air by the left hand and hit by the right hand (p. 20)

11. Volleyball originated in:
    a. USA b. Russia c. Japan (p. 3)

12. If a spiked ball hits the net near the top it will:
    a. bounce directly out
    b. roll down the net and pop out slightly
    c. hang in the net and then drop out (p. 23)

13. If a spiked ball hits the net near the lower edge it will:
    a. bounce directly out
    b. roll down to the tape and pop out
    c. hang in the net and then drop down (p. 23)

14. One tradition which is still basically unchanged in recreational play in the 60 years since the first volleyball tournament is:
    a. 3 hits to a side   b. calling own fouls   c. 15 point game   (p. 4)

TRUE OR FALSE

15. In coed play the girl must hit the ball at least once during the three allowable hits. (p. 2)

16. Even though it appears to be a clean hit, playing a ball below the waist with an open palm is usually considered bad form. (pp. 6-7)

17. You may step on but not over the center line during a rally. (p.13)

18. You may step on but not over the service line while serving. (p. 18)

19. You may step on but not over the side lines during a rally. (p. 13)

20. A ball landing near the top of the net will drop almost straight down. (p. 23)

21. A ball landing near the center of the net will rebound a foot or two before dropping. (p. 23)

22. A "dink" may be directed to fall just behind a block. (p. 7)

23. Screening the server is an important part of offensive strategy. (p. 12)

24. When the defense blocks a spike, contact is considered the first hit for that team. (pp. 1, 13)

25. The spike originated with a team from Manila. (p. 7)

26. A spiked volleyball travels at an average speed of 62 mph. (p. 8)

27. Tumbling techniques have become important in fielding the ball. (pp. 46-47)

28. If you cannot reach the ball with your hand you may field it with your foot. (p. 12)

29. The service area behind each court must be 1.52m square. (p. 10)

30. A volleyball weighs 260-280g and is 65-67cm in diameter. (p. 11)

31. Each team is allowed two time-outs per game. (p. 12)

32. Simultaneous contact of the ball by two teammates constitutes two hits. (p. 12)

33. A ball returned over the cable, outside the court sideline which lands in the opponents court is good. (p. 13)

34. If a back line player leaves his feet to spike a ball closer than 3m to the net he commits a foul. (p. 13)

35. When multiple fouls occur only the first to occur is penalized. (p. 14)

36. A player illegally positioned on the serve commits a foul. (p. 13)

37. A server hitting the ball into the net commits a foul. (p. 13)

38. The referee stops play with a whistle and resumes the play with a second whistle. (p. 15)

39. In doubles play the court is smaller than in the regulation game. (p. 14)

40. The linesmen may not call a serving foul. (p. 16)

41. The umpire is the official in charge of the game. (p. 15)

42. The umpire calls violations regarding position, conduct and substitution. (p. 16)

43. The point is replayed if a double foul occurs. (p. 14)

44. "Throwing" refers to poor ball handling. (p. 9)

45. Balls should have at least 16 panels. (p. 11)

46. A team match consists of the best three out of five games. (p. 12)

47. A match consists of best two out of three games. (p. 12)

48. "Side out" and "rotate" are synonymous. They result in the same action but terms do not mean the same thing. (pp. 2, 15)

49. You may reach over the net to block an opponent's hit if he has hit the ball to return it. (p. 13)

50. The majority of serves falls in the middle third of the receiving team's court. (p. 31)

51. Receiving the serve is an offensive maneuver. (p. 18)

52. The country where volleyball originated has won many world's championships. (p. 5)

53. A back court player who moves to the front court to participate in a block may spike the ball if it has come over the net. (p. 12)

54. If the score is 11-0 a "skunk" is declared and the game is over. (p. 2)

55. A correctly delivered overhand serve is the most difficult to field. (pp. 18-19)

56. Good technique when covering the court requires reaching as far as possible before moving your feet. (p. 22)

57. If a player desires to make a net recovery he should drop down low toward the floor under the ball even though the ball is in the net. (p. 23)

58. The signal caller on offense is usually the setter. (p. 25)

59. A straight arm is desirable for spiking because leading with the elbows slows down the swing. (p. 26)

60. A spike should be executed by driving the heel of the hand directly behind the center of the mass of the ball. (p. 27)

61. Defensive players can relax and rest a little when the play is away from their area. (p. 17)

62. Spiking with the fist is desirable because the ball can be hit harder than with the palm. (p. 27)

63. It is rarely worthwhile to hit the ball over the net on the first or second hit. (p. 28)

64. A volleyball team always has two setters and four spikers on a side. (p. 49)

65. Switching players during play is not permitted in USVBA competition. (pp. 4, 6)

66. A spike which hits a receiver's hands and then bounces off his chest can be set and spiked. (pp. 6, 12)

67. Signalling to other players during play is frowned upon and if you persist in "calling plays" an unsportsmanlike conduct penalty is called. (p. 51)

68. Substitutions can be made only during a dead ball after a request followed by the recognition by an official. (p. 12)

69. A 30-second time out can be followed immediately by a second 30-second time out. (p. 12)

70. A regulation game could finish with a score of 5-3. (p. 12)

71. The team which loses the first game in a match is given the opening serve in the second game. (p. 12)

72. Team rotation always takes place after the team loses its service. (p. 2)

73. A player may stand anywhere behind the back line and serve. (p. 12)

74. It is legal to reach over or under the net during play. (p. 13)

75. It is a foul for a spiker to contact the ball on the opponents' side of the court. (p. 13)

76. A player may not play the ball twice during the time it is on his side of the net. (p. 13)

77. The rules for scoring in doubles are the same as in six man play. (p. 14)

COMPLETION

78. AAU _____ (p. 5)

79. USVBA _____ (p. 5)

80. During a game _____ substitutions are permitted for each team. (p. 12)

81. AIAW_____ (p. 5)

82. The key offensive weapon in volleyball is_____ . (p. 29)

83. The center front player is usually the _____ . (p. 1)

84. The left and right front players are usually the_____ . (p. 29)

85. A received serve should be_____ to the_____ . (p. 1)

86. When front players change positions immediately on the serve it is called _____ . (p. 38)

87. The spiking line is_____ feet from the center line. (pp. 10-11)

88. A regulation volleyball team consists of _____ players.   (p. 1)
89. The service area is _____ feet deep.   (p. 10)

MATCHING

90. Dr. George Fisher	A.	Originator of Volleyball	(p. 3)
91. Julien Lenoir	B.	USVBA Guide	(p. 5)
92. William C. Morgan	C.	International Volleyball Federation	(p. 5)
93. A. G. Spaulding	D.	Original ball	(p. 3)
94. Roundhouse	E.	Delayed contact with ball	(p. 6)
95. Bump	F.	Hard-driven return	(p. 25)
96. Throw	G.	Hand and body contact	(p. 6)
97. Spike	H.	Rebound from arms	(p. 25)
98. Double	I.	Serve or spike	(p. 7)
99. Clean	J.	Distinctly hit	(p. 6)
100. Dink	K.	An offspeed attack	(p. 7)

ANSWERS TO EVALUATION QUESTIONS

Page	Answer and Page Reference
4	William C. Morgan; game intended to be relaxing and less strenuous than basketball; the YMCA instructors learned the game at Springfield College and, over the years, not only introduced it to various YMCA's around the United States but brought the sport to Canada, Central and South America and the Orient; 1964 Olympics in Japan; USVBA, AIWA, NCAA, AAV, YMCA; Volleyball is leading sport in 25 countries, ranks 3rd internationally, and is widely played in schools and recreationally. (pp. 3-5)
8	Court slightly decreased in size; international competition calls for metric measurement since this system is in use almost everywhere except in the United States. (p. 10)
18	No answer.
21	No answer.
22	Step forward to set up player behind and drop right foot back to set up player to the right. (p. 22)
25	No answer.
28	No answer.
31	Middle third of the court; right front court near sideline; receivers should concentrate their players in the area where the serve is most likely to fall. If a server is known to deliver the ball consistently to a certain area, the defense should realign accordingly. (p. 31)
37	Deep sideline and center back court areas, between right front and center back and between left front and center back. (p. 38)
44	No answer.
49	There are four spikers and two setter-spikers; the setter spikers start opposite to each other; they function as spikers when in the front row. (p. 50)
56	By increasing the duration, rate, or intensity of the work; Isokinetic devices permit the resistance to be selectively placed in the range of motion. (pp. 56-57)

KNOWLEDGE TEST ANSWER KEY

Multiple Choice

1. B.	6. B.	11. A.
2. A.	7. A.	12. B.
3. C.	8. B.	13. C.
4. C.	9. A.	14. B.
5. B.	10. C.	

True or False

15. T	26. T	37. T	48. F	58. T	68. T
16. T	27. T	38. T	49. T	59. F	69. T
17. T	28. F	39. T	50. T	60. F	70. T
18. F	29. F	40. F	51. F	61. F	71. F
19. F	30. F	41. F	52. F	62. F	72. F
20. T	31. T	42. T	53. F	63. T	73. F
21. T	32. F	43. T	54. F	64. F	74. F
22. T	33. F	44. T	55. T	65. F	75. T
23. F	34. T	45. F	56. F	66. F	76. F
24. F	35. T	46. T	57. T	67. F	77. F
25. T	36. T	47. T			

Completion

78. American Athletic Union
79. United States Volleyball Association
80. six
81. Association for Inter-collegiate Athletics for Women
82. the spike
83. setter
84. spikers
85. passed/setter
86. switching
87. 10
88. six
89. six

Matching

90. B		96. E
91. C		97. F
92. A		98. G
93. D		99. J
94. I		100. K
95. H		

index